# Smallholding
# Manual

## Credits

| | |
|---|---|
| **Author:** | **Liz Shankland** |
| **Project Manager:** | **Louise McIntyre** |
| **Copy editor:** | **Jane Hutchings** |
| **Page design:** | **Rod Teasdale** |
| **Illustrations:** | **Dominic Stickland** |
| **Photography:** | **All photography by the author, unless otherwise indicated on page.** |
| **Library photos:** | **Alamy photos on pages 38, 82 (all), 83 (all except top right), 142** |

First published in 2012

A catalogue record for this book is available from the British Library

ISBN 978 0 85733 225 7

Published by Haynes Publishing, Sparkford, Yeovil, Somerset BA22 7JJ, UK
Tel: 01963 442030 Fax: 01963 440001
Int. tel: +44 1963 442030 Int. fax: +44 1963 440001
E-mail: sales@haynes.co.uk
Website: www.haynes.co.uk

Haynes North America Inc.
861 Lawrence Drive, Newbury Park,
California 91320, USA

Printed and bound in the USA

## Author acknowledgements

Writing a book can become an all-consuming affair, and it often gets to the stage where everything else has to be put on hold if it's ever to see the light of day. With this in mind, my heartfelt sympathies go out to my husband, Gerry Toms, who has had to live with me writing this, my third book, and my second Haynes Manual. I'm indebted to him, not only for his patience – which, understandably, was tested to the limit at times – but also for his help with various sections of the book, and particularly when I needed a sounding board for ideas.

Life throws up all kinds of hurdles, and the staff at Haynes have been incredibly understanding throughout. I'm grateful to Project Manager Louise McIntyre for bearing with me and I trust she didn't have too many regrets about working with me a second time.

Thanks are also due to my trusty fencing contractor Paul Davies, who diverted his team off another job in order to construct a run of fencing for the step-by-step project featured in Chapter 4 – I just hope the materials and labour aren't added to my next bill!

# Smallholding
# Manual

## THE COMPLETE STEP-BY-STEP GUIDE

**LIZ SHANKLAND**          FOREWORD BY **KATE HUMBLE**

# CONTENTS

# FOREWORD

I moved to Wales with my husband in the winter of 2007. We were both excited and nervous in equal measure to be moving from a terraced London house to an old stone farmhouse with four and half acres of land.

We already had chickens. Not by choice. The people we bought our house from had asked us to 'chicken-sit' until they were settled in to their new place. So, on our very first morning I found myself walking through the frost with a bucket of grain and standing entranced by Rhodri the cockerel and his harem of pretty hens eagerly pecking up the food I had provided. I filled their water bowl, cleaned out the chicken house and it struck me that this was a pretty perfect way to start a day.

A month or so later, Rhodri and his girls were reclaimed by their rightful owners and we felt bereft. We went to a neighbour who bred chickens and bought three hens. A friend had an unwanted cockerel (there are lots of those about) and as we'd read that hens rather like the company of a handsome strutting male, we decided to adopt Roger. He was swiftly followed by Gary the gander and his two ladies.

We were given some Aylesbury ducks. We got slightly drunk at a dinner party and woke up to discover we had agreed to buy two KuneKune piglets. We went to the local horse and pony rescue centre and came away with two donkeys. We dug a vegetable garden, built a wildlife pond, spent all our money on animal feed and realised that going on holiday had become very difficult indeed. In short, somehow, we'd become smallholders.

If you don't like getting up early, having mud on every item of clothing you own, lying awake at night worrying whether or not the ram you've borrowed fancies your ewes, then smallholding – and this book – isn't for you. If none of that scares you, and you love the idea of collecting your own eggs, eating your own sausages and roasting a chicken that didn't come from a supermarket, then I urge you to give it a go.

**Kate Humble**

# INTRODUCTION

**Where do you think most people would choose to live if money was no object? According to research, the majority don't hanker after an enormous footballers' wives-style mansion with all the mod cons and luxuries: the typical dream home is a newly-built, detached, four-bedroom house in a rural location with about half an acre of land.**

According to the website www.gocompare.com, the perfect property would also have to be within easy reach of a school, shop, post office and pub. The survey didn't ask any questions about whether those interviewed wanted to live 'the good life', grow their own vegetables or raise their own livestock. Nevertheless, the results do prove something: most of us want our own rural idyll away from the hustle and bustle of city life, and we'd also like a little bit of land to separate and protect us from the rest of the world.

I'd wager that the majority of people who move to the country aren't hell-bent on living a self-sufficient lifestyle. It's more a question of living a better lifestyle, one with less pressure, more pleasure, and more time to enjoy life. And, for most people, it's not about making money off the land – it's more about being happy.

Liz at her hilltop smallholding with the dogs Gordon, Stella and Bryn – and, of course, some pigs.

With that in mind, I hope this book will be of some use to you – whether you're trying to decide if smallholding is for you, embarking on the search for your perfect place, or planning what you want to do with your newly purchased land. Don't treat this book as a prescriptive 'how it must be done' manual. Apart from the legal and welfare obligations, you have a free hand to do things as you wish. I'd prefer you to use the Haynes Smallholding Manual as a 'how it can be done' guide. Every smallholding is unique, and we all have different aims and objectives, so there's no definitive blueprint.

If you take the plunge and become a smallholder, just remember to enjoy it. Don't rush into things and commit yourself to projects you aren't ready for, nor overstretch yourself – physically or financially. Never forget that what you're aiming to do is to make a better life for yourself and those around you. If it becomes a chore instead of a pleasure, you're either doing it wrong, or it's time to get out.

We all have a reason for wanting to up-sticks and change our lives: it could be a long-held dream to provide a degree of self-sufficiency for yourself and your family; the decision may be prompted by a change in personal or working circumstances; occasionally, a property with land will become available, presenting an opportunity that is just too hard to resist; or there may come a morning when you wake up and decide you want to do something completely different.

I'm sometimes embarrassed to admit that my own journey into smallholding bore no resemblance to any of those scenarios. It began on impulse and, although I wouldn't recommend my rash and reckless course of action to anyone, I don't regret it for one minute.

It all happened very quickly. I was working full-time in the media in a very satisfying job, the only downside of which was that I spent most of my waking hours either at work in Bristol or commuting from my home in Wales. As the only available parking around the BBC building in Bristol was in residential areas, it was a case of 'who dares wins', so I would be out of bed before most milkmen and would end up at work hours before I needed to be there. At the end of the day, I would hang on until the city traffic had eased and then wend my way home, listening to *The Archers* and trying to decide which ready meal to pull out of the freezer for dinner.

One summer evening, after a particularly busy day and a frustratingly long commute, I found myself browsing through the local paper with a gin and tonic in hand. I turned the page to the property ads, and there was the picture that would change my life. It was a very tired-looking old farmhouse, but it caught my eye for a variety of reasons.

Firstly, it was an unusually large house with three storeys and quirky architectural features. Secondly, it looked neglected and in need of serious restoration; it almost shouted, 'Rescue me!' Thirdly, it came with land, and as a passionate gardener I'd always wanted a big garden. Finally, and probably most importantly at the time, it was only about three miles away. Properties like this never came up for sale so close to home; the only ones I'd seen advertised were normally a good three hours' drive away from where I worked, and so out of the question.

I showed it to my husband Gerry – more out of surprise than anything else – and he suggested we take a look. Within minutes, we were making our way up a single-track road and pulling into the deserted farmyard. We decided on the spot that we would arrange a viewing.

I must admit that the whole idea was completely crazy. We were doing no more than being nosey. For a start, we weren't even looking for a house – let alone a smallholding. For the past three years we'd spent everything we earned and every spare hour we possessed modernising a 1970s house and turning its gardens into a wildlife paradise, complete with ponds and interesting plants, and – in keeping with horticultural fashion of the time – timber decking from which to view it all. Alan Titchmarsh would have been impressed. We were looking forward to our first summer sitting in our little leafy oasis, doing nothing more strenuous than reading the papers and maybe hosting the occasional barbecue.

So, after spending year after year practically living in a building site, why on earth would we want to start all over again – this time taking on a renovation job of such massive proportions that even Kevin McCloud of *Grand Designs* would turn it down?

I think Gerry and I both knew that we wanted a change of some kind. As townies working in busy cities, we were happiest when we were working together outdoors (digging a pond in a snowstorm on Easter Monday proved that to us) and we felt ready to take on an adventure.

When we looked round the farmhouse we realised we wanted the place more than we'd ever wanted anything before. We didn't mess around making offers below the asking price – we agreed to pay the full whack and that was that.

With hindsight, it was a ridiculous move and we stretched ourselves to the limit financially, but we just had to find ways of making ends meet. We were totally unprepared, had no plans whatsoever, and no idea of what we might do with the land. We had no intention of keeping livestock, and neither of us had any experience of dealing with any animals other than the usual domestic pets.

It didn't take long for us to acquire some hens. Then

Roxy the orphaned lamb who became one of the family.

came ducks and turkeys and, eventually, the 'serious' livestock – goats, sheep and pigs. Pigs were to become the focus of the holding. We began by buying in weaners – eight-week-old piglets – two at a time and rearing them for pork, but I quickly got the bug. After trying various breeds, I decided that Tamworths were my favourite, so I went to a good breeder and bought two registered pedigree gilts as the foundation of my herd.

Once I started breeding my own stock, I was persuaded into showing – a practice that was to become a bit of an obsession. I now tour the UK every year, exhibiting at between eight and ten major agricultural shows. My sows have won the UK Tamworth Champion of Champions competition two years running, as well as taking championship titles in prestigious inter-breed contests. I'm delighted with the standard of my herd and so are my customers, some of whom travel hundreds of miles to my hilltop holding in Caerphilly, South Wales, to buy breeding stock or weaners to raise for meat.

The way I got into smallholding isn't one I'd recommend – quite the opposite, in fact – and that's one of the reasons I wanted to write this book. If I'd done some research instead of plunging headfirst into something I knew nothing about, I think I would have achieved success much sooner, and probably with a lot less expense and frustration. I hope others will be able to benefit from the experience and knowledge I've gained along the way.

Good luck, and happy smallholding.

**Liz Shankland**

# WHY TAKE ON A SMALLHOLDING?

Why would anyone want a smallholding? For a whole host of reasons, some of which may be practical, others totally impractical. It may be that you simply want a *cordon sanitaire* – a 'buffer zone' – if you like, between you and the rest of the world.

Wanting to escape from the city and enjoy the peace and quiet of rural life is nothing new. People have been hankering after the same thing for generations. However, more and more people now want the best of both worlds; rather than give up their well-paid jobs, they would like to keep the comfortable income, but enjoy a better quality of life. Of course, there will always be those who want the complete lifestyle and career change, and who will have plans to start a business or explore a new world of possibilities.

### Is the decision yours alone?

If it's just you embarking on this adventure – or if you have a partner who is equally committed to the idea – then that should make the project a lot easier. But the more people there are who would be affected by the move, the more complicated it's likely to be.

Carolyn Ekins

Children can be a real stumbling block. The smaller they are, the easier and more adaptable they should be, but when you are dealing with stubborn teenagers who have a close network of friends, favourite haunts and pastimes, the process of uprooting the family is likely to be problematical. Think of the prospect of extracting them from their comfortable lifestyle and moving them to a possibly decrepit house, miles from anywhere, which does not have central heating or – horror of horrors – broadband.

**Questions to ask yourself**

## Would everyone be happy to move to the countryside?

Older children will certainly have reservations, but even partners may harbour some nagging doubts that they're unsure about voicing. Think also about the impact on elderly parents and other relatives. It's better to get everyone's opinions out in the open before going too far.

## Do you really want to be a landowner?

Would it be better to buy a rural cottage which would give you a life in the countryside, but not burden you with the responsibility of looking after land or livestock? If you're a keen horse rider and have plans to buy your own horse and build stables, maybe renting a paddock or finding a livery yard would be a better option. Finally – and probably most importantly – are you dissatisfied with your current job or your relationship and in need of a challenge or a fresh start? Buying a smallholding will certainly be a distraction from your problems, but it won't necessarily solve them.

## Could you give up life's little comforts?

Would you mind being miles away from the supermarket, the pub, the DVD store, or the Indian takeaway? Popping in for a drink at the nearest 'local' could mean taking the car, so that long-awaited pint might have to be a pint of lemonade.

## Do you have the time and energy for a smallholding?

Should you decide to keep your job and look after the smallholding as a hobby, could you honestly say you'd have the energy and enthusiasm at the end of a working day to start work all over again? And how would others in your life think about being deprived of your time and attention?

Land does not look after itself. Pastureland left untended can soon become swamped by dock, nettles, creeping buttercup and more. If you're determined to grow crops or raise livestock, you may have to buy in some help. Could you afford to?

Also, what would happen if you fell ill, wanted a holiday, or had to go away for work? Who would take over? You need to have a Plan B that covers all eventualities.

# Financing the move

Once you've decided that smallholding is definitely for you, the next big thing to consider is how you'll afford it.

If you're selling a property in one of the more expensive parts of the UK and moving to a cheaper area, money might not be too much of a problem, as you may be able to buy your new home for cash. For most people, however, that won't be an option. The majority will have to take out a mortgage and will need to carry on working – either full or part-time – in order to pay off the debt and all the usual bills.

## The options

So what are the options open to you? You might like to consider the following suggestions and also the potential problems.

| SUGGESTIONS | DRAWBACKS |
|---|---|
| **Keep your old job and commute.** | It could mean a long, expensive, and tiring journey at either end of the day, and you may still have to work on the smallholding when you get home. |
| **Look for a new job in your new location.** | There may not be a demand for what you have to offer; your dream home may be cheap because good jobs are scarce and wages are low. |
| **Work from home – either freelancing or setting up a completely new business, maybe involving a hobby or a particular skill.** | Working from home might not be an option because of the type of work you do. Becoming self-employed can be a daunting and complicated prospect and working from home requires discipline and dedication. If you're used to working alongside others you may find it lonely. Demand for your work might fluctuate – along with your income. You may need to invest in an office, workshop, tools or equipment – and you may also need planning permission. |
| **Try to make money out of your smallholding by selling your own produce.** | Firstly, you need to find markets for your produce, and depending on the economic climate, that may not be easy. If you plan to sell from a farm shop, you may need to invest in the right facilities and be prepared to have customers calling at your door at all hours of the day. You'll need land management or livestock handling skills, or be willing to acquire some. Don't forget that farming can be extremely physically demanding, and you may have to spend long hours in cold, wet and miserable conditions. If you keep livestock, you'll have to be prepared for dealing with sickness and death, and you may even have to learn to kill in the case of an emergency. |
| **Buy an existing rural business as a going concern.** | Again, if times are hard, and unless you find a niche market or are a real whizz at marketing, you may struggle. If the business isn't already a success, you could be buying yourself into trouble. |
| **One of you keeps the old job, while the other tries one of the above.** | You are almost certain to suffer a drop in income. The partner carrying on in normal employment may feel resentful of the other. |

Consider how much you may have to spend on renovations.

Stepping into someone else's shoes may be an option, but be sure you know what you're doing.

## Financial planning

Above all, you have to make sure you can afford what you're getting into.

Whether you like it or not, you have to do some 'number-crunching'. Make a list of all your outgoings, future commitments, and income, or projected income. It really is the only way to discover whether you'll be able to make ends meet or not, and it's also an excellent way of assessing your regular spending and determining whether some thing are essential or not.

Work out what you owe, look at the monthly repayments you make and any other unavoidable outgoings such as food, travel, insurance, subscriptions. Allow some additional costs for, say, clothes, entertainment, hobbies and interests. Make two columns – one headed 'What I need' and the other, 'What I want'. Be ruthless and realistic.

Holidays might have to go on hold for a while.

# FINDING THE PERFECT PLACE

Despite slumps elsewhere in the property market, at the time of writing farmland is still managing to hold its own, and demand for anything from small plots and pony paddocks to vast commercial farms encompassing several thousands of acres has continued to rise.

FOR SALE
CONVERTED BARN
WITH 3 ACRES OF LAND
& SWIMMING POOL
UPTO 9 ACRES OF
FLAT PASTURE LAND
ALL ENQUIRIES
07970 434676
600 YARDS DOWN THE LANE
1st LEFT

Statistics released in 2011 by the Royal Institution of Chartered Surveyors – which publishes regular surveys on market trends – revealed that farmland prices had reached an all-time high as demand for land outstripped availability. The average price per acre in the UK was estimated at more than £6,000, the RICS report said. Whereas demand from smallholders and horse fans had helped to push up prices in previous years, the more recent rise was due to increasing demand from commercial farmers looking to expand production in response to better commodity prices.

Whatever the true market value of land, the reality is that if a number of would-be purchasers are equally determined to snare a particular farm or smallholding, the resulting bidding war can cause the price to soar. At the end of the day, it comes down to that big question: how much is it worth to you?

Whether you're looking for a 'normal' place to live, or searching for your ultimate rural idyll, finding your dream home is rarely an easy process. Buying a house or flat can be complicated enough, and the period from making an offer to moving in can be fraught with problems, but buying a smallholding is even more of a minefield.

## Choosing a location

The key to finding what you want is to start off with a clear idea of what that is.

**Here are some points to get you thinking:**

- How important is the geographical location? Does your work depend on you being within a specific commuting distance, or are you sufficiently flexible to consider places possibly further afield?
- Do you need or want to be based close to major towns or cities, with easy access to motorways or public transport?
- Is it important to be within walking distance of schools, shops, local amenities?
- Would you mind living in an isolated position (particularly if yourself or your partner will be home alone at times)?
- Have you considered the cost of investing in a 4x4, should you choose a remote location?
- How do you feel about prominent visual features? Would you mind a pylon a few metres away from your front door? What if there was a rubbish dump, a scrapyard, or a travellers' site close by?
- If you dream of selling produce at the farm gate, do you need to be near a main road?
- Would neighbours' activities upset you, or might some of your plans conflict with theirs? For example, would you mind if a milk tanker blocked the road every day for half an hour? Similarly, if you started up a large-scale free-range egg operation, would your neighbours object to the smell or noise?
- How does the current owner get on with the neighbours? Are there any boundary disputes? The vendor has a legal duty to tell you.
- How would you feel about a shared access? Would you have to pay towards maintaining the road or track?

- If you're considering a major move, for instance, to a different country with its own language and culture, how would you feel about being considered an 'incomer' – and how prepared would you be to work at integrating into the local community?

## Buildings, services and regulations

- It's essential to determine whether there's an agricultural tie on the holding. This will lower the selling price, but will also limit residency to someone whose primary income is derived from agricultural or horticultural activities. Currently, equine businesses, such as livery yards and riding schools, don't qualify. It may look as if you may be making a big saving, but could you satisfy the criteria? There are numerous companies which will attempt to overturn agricultural restrictions, but it can be a mistake to buy before you're sure of success.

- If there's a house, is it in a decent condition? If not, are you prepared for major renovation work and the time, inconvenience and costs involved?

- What about essential services? Does the property have mains electricity, water, and sewerage? Your water may have to come from a bore-hole or a spring. Your household waste might flow into a septic tank, which would need to be pumped out at regular intervals. There may just be an ancient soak-away system, which could get blocked at times. Could you fix it yourself, if you had to?

- Does the property have suitable outbuildings? How much would it cost to build what you need – and could you get planning permission? Consider what might happen if you couldn't get consent.

- If you plan to run a business, you may need planning permission for a change of use. Might you have to create a new access, which could require planning permission?

- Does the land have any buildings of architectural or historical importance – maybe even with Listed status? If so, any repairs or modifications will have to be carried out with the approval of the relevant conservation organisation, such as English Heritage or Cadw in Wales (see Further information, page 172). Also, if there's an ancient monument on the land, you may be required to give access to the general public.

## The land

- Is the land in good condition, or would it require a lot of work to improve? Land in the UK is graded from 1 (best) to 5 (worst), and if your plans involve growing crops, this is an important factor to consider.

- How well-drained is the land? Is the soil light and chalky and so lacking in nutrients, or is it heavy clay, turning into a mudbath after rain? Is there any likelihood of serious flooding? Check with the Environment Agency (see Further information, page 172).

- How stony is the soil? If it's full of rocks and boulders, that could rule out cultivation for crops and also make the job of digging holes for fence and gate posts a nightmare.

- Which direction does the land face? Don't forget that a south-facing plot will get more sun. How exposed is the site, and how strong are the prevailing winds?

- Does the land have a reliable water supply, or could one be connected? Whether you're intent on growing crops or keeping livestock, you will need irrigation.

- How would you feel if there were public rights of way across your fields? You could have strangers walking over your land, or even through your garden. You may have to look after footpaths and stiles, and possibly install extra fencing to keep walkers and their dogs separate from your livestock.

- On the subject of containing livestock, does the property already have adequate fencing and/or hedging, or is there work to be done – and at what cost?

- Is there easy vehicle access from main highways, or would you have to use rough, maybe winding and narrow lanes?

- Are there any environmental constraints on the land? Is all or some of it designated a Site of Special Scientific Interest (SSSI), or subject to other conditions imposed to protect habitat or special features?
- Does the bulk of the land adjoin the house and garden, or is it detached and maybe separated by a road or a neighbour's land? This could be an issue when it comes to security, with regard to keeping an eye on livestock, buildings, or equipment.

## Acres/hectares

Land is normally measured by the acre, which is 4,166 sq m, but you will often see it described in hectares. One hectare (ha) measures about 2.4 acres.

## How much land?

Size isn't everything! A few acres of good-quality, level, free-draining land can often be worth more than 25 acres (10 ha) of largely steep, rocky ground, which is impossible to cultivate. Don't get too carried away by the acreage of a property on paper, because large swathes may, for instance, be too boggy to work with.

Location and local demand will influence prices enormously. In many affluent areas estate agents are seeing tiny pony paddocks being sold for as much as small farms, simply because scraps of land with good road access so rarely come onto the market.

But how much land do your really *need*? Well, how long is a piece of string? You may be content with a house surrounded by an acre or less if all you want is a bit of privacy, somewhere for the children and the dog to play, a vegetable patch and a few chickens.

If your plans are more ambitious, you will have numerous factors to consider, including location, climate, and, of course, your budget. It would help to work out how much of a smallholder you want to be. Do you want to be totally self-sufficient and produce all your own food and fuel, or would you just like to produce key elements of your diet, such as meat and vegetables?

As touched upon earlier, the better the location, climate and soil quality, the less land you will need. Also, depending on how well you manage the land, it's feasible to run a productive smallholding on a very small acreage. Many people with smaller-sized plots are more careful and economical with the way they use what is available, in order to achieve maximum results.

The demand for equine properties remains high.

# How to use the land

If you asked a dozen smallholders how they would use a patch of land of a given size, you would get more than a dozen different suggestions. Here are just a few ideas, looking at three holdings of varying sizes. To make things simpler, let's say that each one is a lowland holding in an area that has average rainfall and decent, but not outstanding soil.

## EXAMPLE 1:
## 0.5 TO 1 ACRE

- A large fruit and vegetable plot and a few fruit trees – along with a greenhouse or small polytunnel to supply produce all year round
- A pond with ducks – for eggs and/or meat
- A dozen or so chickens or other birds for eggs and/or meat
- Beehives for the production of honey and other products – and also to help pollinate fruit and vegetable crops
- A garage/workshop/office (could be used as a food preparation area/dairy/butchery or as a farm shop)

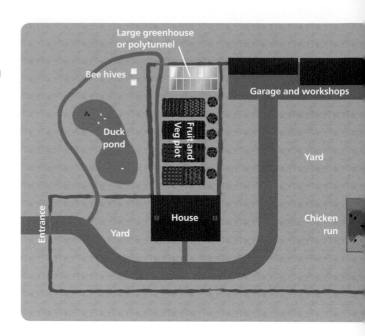

## EXAMPLE 2:
## 5 ACRES

All of the features included in Example 1, plus:
- Fodder crops for livestock
- An orchard
- Additional outbuildings

- A spare paddock for isolation of stock – for quarantine; for injured animals; for temporarily segregating sexes; as a lambing/nursery area; as emergency grazing in case of waterlogged ground.

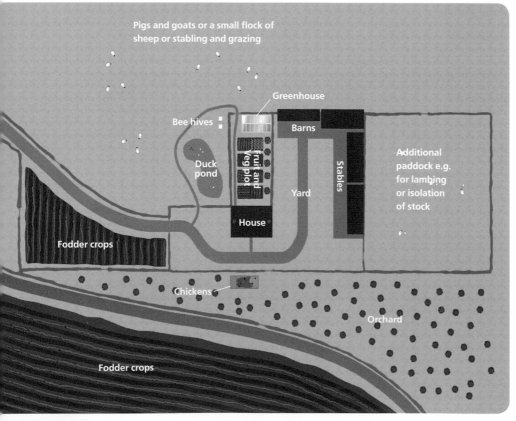

**PLUS ONE OF THE FOLLOWING OPTIONS:**

EITHER

**a)**
- A few weaners to be reared for pork or bacon and to provide manure for the vegetable patch. AND
- Some goats to produce milk (for you and for the pigs), possibly meat for the table, and more manure. OR

**b)**
- A small breeding flock of sheep (no more than a dozen). OR

**c)**
- A small herd of breeding pigs (e.g. two sows plus litters). OR

**d)**
- Stabling and grazing for a few horses, llamas, or alpacas. OR

**e)**
- Fields for grazing or crops for hire to neighbouring farmers.

## EXAMPLE 3:
## 10 ACRES

All listed in Example 1, plus your choice from Example 2, plus:

- Two cows and calves – for milk, meat, and manure
- Additional paddocks for rotation of stock
- Further outbuildings – for overwintering livestock, storage of fodder and machinery
- More fodder crops for your livestock or to sell to others

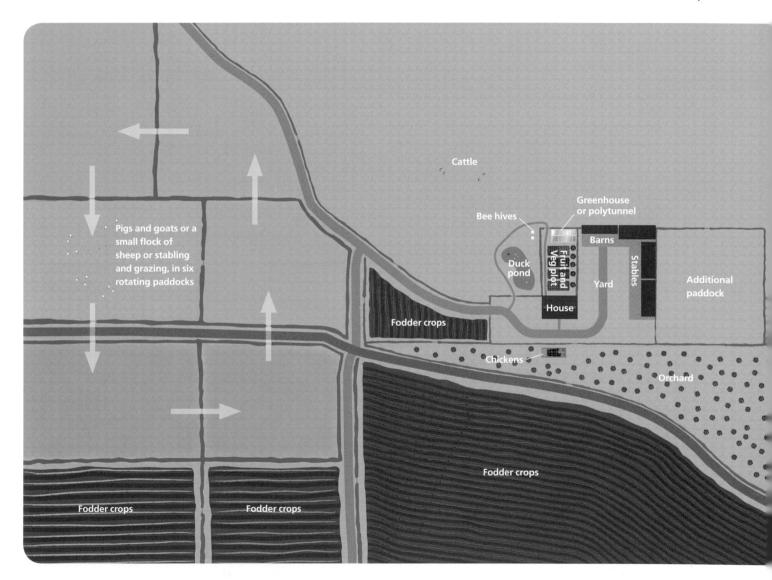

It must be emphasised that the illustrations shown are purely suggestions of what can be accommodated. It's extremely important not to underestimate how much land you will need, particularly if you're taking on livestock. It's often surprising how quickly grass and other vegetation gets eaten and how easily land gets trampled into a quagmire. For both these reasons, you have to have sufficient land in order to rotate your animals, allow damaged paddocks to recover, and to get round the problem of buying in fodder to supplement what they have available. But food supply isn't the only factor here: to ensure healthy livestock, you have to be able to move them to fresh ground on a regular basis.

Over-grazing the same area of land will increase parasitic worm burden in the soil. On the other hand, under-grazing can be detrimental to grassland, and can also devalue its benefit to wildlife. Grass that isn't grazed efficiently or cut at appropriate times will quickly revert to scrub. It's worth taking tips from experienced farmers or professional agricultural consultants to design an effective grassland management regime.

## Finding your smallholding

Lots of time can be wasted viewing properties that are completely unsuitable for your needs. Estate agents who get you on their books will often feed your details into a computer system that will send you information on a whole host of inappropriate smallholdings. It pays to be extremely prescriptive when describing your 'wish list' of desirable features, but you will almost certainly also have to do your own research.

You will have a rough idea of where you want to live, the type of property you want and, by now, you should have a list of your top priorities and preferences, so it's time to start whittling things down and finding what you want.

### SOURCES OF INFORMATION

The Internet has taken the business of selling property to a whole new level. Estate agents all have websites, and more and more enterprising home owners have cottoned on to the fact that they may be able to sell their properties themselves – either by setting up a dedicated website or by posting on a specialist smallholders' forum – saving themselves estate agent's fees. It pays to surf around and see what is available (see Further information, page 172, for suggestions).

Local newspapers are a useful starting point, too. Most weekly papers have a property section which, as well as featuring the leading estate agents in the area, will include private advertisements as well. Once you have narrowed down your search to a few key areas, find out the names of the local papers and ask for them to be sent to you each week. It will probably cost you less than £1 a week for each paper.

One big benefit of buying the local rag is that, as well as getting the property advertisements, you will also have news from the community you are considering moving into. Keeping up with the local news can be extremely useful, as

Plans for the proposed site were first unveiled in January 2009, with Covanta claiming the incinerator would create up to 600 jobs

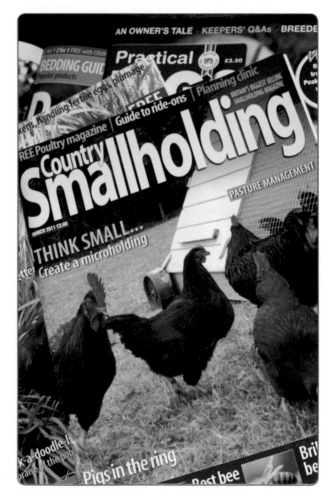

you can learn more about those areas where your shortlisted properties are located. You may also be forewarned about anything from planning decisions and major developments taking place to public transport plans or big investments in industry or the local economy – any of which might influence your decision about buying. The more information you can glean in advance, the better.

Most papers will have their own websites, but you're unlikely to be given access to every story in the paper. It's far more likely to be the main stories that are posted on the site, so you'd be better off investing in a weekly subscription.

Specialist smallholding and countryside magazines can also be a useful place to look for properties for sale, and you're likely to find several independent advertisements, paid for by the vendors themselves.

### SEEKING OUT ESTATE AGENTS

As mentioned earlier, buying a smallholding can be much more complicated than simply buying a house. Most high street estates agents will only occasionally get a smallholding or a farm on their books, so you need to look for those which specialise in rural properties. Go back to the local papers, and check out which agencies appear to be the most well-suited to the task.

If you lead a busy life, what you don't want from an estate agent is a regular flurry of brochures or emails about properties that don't meet your needs, so make sure right from the start that the agency knows exactly what you want. If you're too vague and, for instance, say that you want a house 'with land', you could end up receiving information on everything from houses with large gardens to massive farms that are out of your price range. The more specific you are, the easier the job will be – for you and for the estate agents you choose to deal with. The best way of getting what you want is to keep in regular contact with the agents, let them know you are serious, and build up a rapport.

The local Post Office can be a good source of local information.

### NARROWING DOWN THE SEARCH

Viewing potential homes takes time, so work out in advance which ones on your list you really want to visit. After all, if your current home is hundreds of miles away, you want to make sure you won't be wasting your time.

Ring the estate agents and question them relentlessly about the location of a property, its proximity to shops and other amenities, to the extent that you can build up a mental picture of what it would be like driving up to it. The office is likely to be staffed by people who live locally, so they should know the area well. Think also about ringing the local Post Office, too – if the area still has one.

Ordnance Survey maps are a great source of information – whether you have a paper version or choose to view online. They are incredibly detailed and will show you features on or close to properties, which may be of interest. Similarly, Google Earth is an excellent resource, providing satellite pictures of land and buildings and giving you more of a feel for a location than an estate agent's particulars ever could.

### VIEWING PROPERTIES

In all the excitement of viewing properties, it's easy to get distracted. It is worth going back to the beginning of this chapter and constructing a checklist of things you want and don't want. Take a copy with you and make notes as you go along, and ask the estate agent or vendor if you can take photographs, or even video footage, to jog your memory later on.

You might want to check the availability of local schools.

Don't be surprised if you end up on a group viewing. As smallholdings in prime locations get increasingly scarce, estate agents are becoming keen on lumping all prospective buyers together – possibly to cut down on the number of viewings, for the vendor's benefit, but more likely to encourage an air of competition among the punters. After all, if you know someone else is interested in the same thing as you, you want it all the more – right?

Group viewings are never the best way of seeing a house, so try and arrange a second, private visit.

Next stop after touring the property and land is the local pub – for a little more research about the property you have just seen and the area in general. Find out how long it takes to drive to key destinations like hospitals, schools and shops, and gather information on what the area is like in extreme weather, particularly when it snows.

## MAKING A DECISION

Sit down, dig out that checklist, and carefully go through each of the points you made. There will always plenty more smallholdings out there, so don't feel you have to rush into a decision. If you do decide to go for it, get yourself a good solicitor who has experience of handling transactions involving rural and agricultural properties. Once again, remember that you are not buying a normal home, so find a specialist who knows the pitfalls.

Try the corner shop for more helpful hints about the area.

A drink in the local could help you make your mind up.

# Preparing for your move

**Everyone wants a stress-free move, so plan well and make life easier for yourself. Make a list of things you need to do as moving day approaches, in order of priority.**

How far ahead you start your countdown will depend on your circumstances and how much you have to organise – three months before the expected completion date should be ample time. Do yourself a big favour and have a good sort out. Get rid of all the junk and clutter – whether you sell it on the Internet or at car boot sales, or just give it to a charity shop, you'll feel a whole lot better.

## Getting ready for your new life

If you have been planning your move for some time, you will probably have sourced some good books about running a smallholding, growing produce and rearing livestock. If you haven't, take a look at the recommended reading list (see Further information, page 172), where you will also find a list of useful websites, magazines and other sources of information.

It may seem an age between agreeing to buy and actually moving in, but something useful you can do while you're waiting is to sketch out your ideas for your holding and make a list of priority jobs. Do you need to get fencing done, or hedges laid or planted, for instance? Now is the time to work out what needs to be done and how much it'll cost you.

Let a charity shop benefit from your clear out.

It's likely that you'll have a rough plan of the land from the estate agent's particulars, which will include field sizes. If you don't, arrange to have the land measured. Then you will be able to work out the quantities of materials needed, so you can start telephoning local suppliers and contractors for prices.

Do you want to erect outbuildings, improve or change the use of existing structures? Get in touch with the council's planning department to see whether you need permission. If keeping livestock is part of your plan, think about the kind of accommodation and equipment you'll need, where you're going to source it, how long it will take to arrive, and the costs involved. Do the same for livestock – contact breeders well in advance and place orders. Good-quality animals – and particularly rare breeds – are often in great demand.

Think about joining a farming union or a smallholders' association, if there is one. They can help with everything from advice on specialist insurance cover to applying to join agri-environment schemes. It is definitely worth using some of this 'in limbo' time to investigate any financial help that might be on offer – whether from the government or other sources, such as environmental organisations.

Car boot sales are a great way of de-cluttering.

## CHECKLIST

www.pickfords.co.uk

### Things to do well in advance

- Book a removal company (or a self-drive vehicle). If you can't find a removal firm by personal recommendation, look for one that belongs to the British Association of Removers or the National Guild of Removers and Storers.
- Get some strong boxes and pack valuables and things you won't need in the near future. List the contents on the outside of the box to help easy sorting.
- Start looking for the best deals in electricity, gas or oil for your new home.

Remember to mark boxes clearly.

### A month before moving

- Start sending people your new address.
- Arrange to get your mail redirected.
- Begin some serious packing – and don't forget to label the boxes!
- Stop shopping and start eating your way through the contents of your freezer and food cupboards.

### A week or two before moving

- Arrange for friends and relatives to help you move, or to look after children or pets.
- Defrost the fridge and freezer.
- Cancel milk and newspaper deliveries and settle bills.
- Keep in touch with your estate agent and solicitor to make sure everything is going smoothly.
- Confirm arrangements with the removal or van hire firm.
- Arrange insurance cover for the new place, including outbuildings.

### The day before moving

- Pack a box of essentials – tea and coffee-making items, kettle, toilet rolls, light bulbs, bed linen. Don't put these in the removal van, keep them with you, along with any valuables or important documents.

If you plan to erect new buildings, seek advice on planning regulations well in advance.

If your land is not already registered as an agricultural holding (see Legal Requirements, page 34), apply for a County Parish Holding number. Also, if you are hoping to run your smallholding as a business, explore the pros and cons of registering for VAT. Depending on the nature of the business, you may find you can claim back quite significant sums involved in setting up your enterprise.

## Getting some training

Doing your homework and getting some experience under your belt is essential, so find some training courses to master any skills you might need. Locate the nearest agricultural college and see what courses it offers. Many colleges will run tailor-made smallholder courses, which will give you an overview of everything from land management to livestock handling, while others may only run one- or two-day sessions on particular subjects, or more formal training courses, which will give you recognised qualifications.

Courses in traditional rural skills, such as hedge-laying and drystone walling, are extremely useful. If your local agricultural college does not cater for such things, try conservation organisations such as the British Trust for Conservation Volunteers or the Wildlife Trusts. They often offer training opportunities to volunteers and organise work parties so you can hone your skills under supervision before you have to go it alone.

It may also be worth getting in touch with Lantra, an independent skills agency for the land-based and environmental sector in the UK. The organisation works with colleges and other training providers to provide courses for farming families and employees, often at discounted prices. You will, however, have to satisfy a list of criteria, as the courses are aimed more at those employed full-time in a particular industry.

There is an increasing number of enterprising smallholders running their own training courses. These can be great value, but they can also be incredibly expensive for what you actually get. For a lot of people, price and travelling distance will be the two main deciding factors when choosing such a course – but what about the quality of the training? Find out the following:

### TOP TIP

### HANDS-ON WORK EXPERIENCE

A good way of getting some experience and benefiting from the knowledge of an experienced person is to seek out a friendly farmer or smallholder who might be prepared to let you spend some time observing and helping out. As long as you are happy to get your hands dirty and play farm labourer, you could learn a lot. Even everyday husbandry tasks can seem a little daunting when you are alone with only a book to work from, but being able to try your hand at various jobs under the watchful eye of someone who has done it all countless times before can be a great way to learn.

Learning how to reverse a trailer correctly is money well spent.

- How qualified is the course tutor? How much relevant experience does he or she have? If the course is run by a relative beginner, how sound is their knowledge?
- What will you be taught on the course? Find out exactly what will be covered and see if it suits your needs.
- How 'hands-on' is the course? If, for instance, the course involves animal husbandry, will you have the chance to get involved and attempt various tasks like handling, tagging and injecting, or will the tutor merely be demonstrating?
- How many people will be in your group? Too many and you may not have time to ask questions or get the chance to try out a technique.
- Will there be course materials to take away? There may be handouts summarising the day's activities or giving more information, but not all courses will include these.

If you do get a place on one of these courses, don't order livestock or equipment on impulse, because you may find out later that you have paid more than the going rate. You may be tempted to buy everything you need at this 'one-stop shop', but it pays to shop around before committing yourself.

Learn about animal husbandry tasks before you need to do them yourself.

## CONTACT DETAILS

**For details of the organisations mentioned, see Further information, page 172.**

# VETERINARY MEDICINE RECO

| Date of purchase | Drug, batch ID, and quantity purchased | Name and address of supplier | Date treatment started | Date treatment finished | Date when withdrawal ended | Identity and number of animals treated |
|---|---|---|---|---|---|---|
| 24/10/10 | Dectomax 50ml | Tyndale Veterinary Practice | 30/10/10 | 30/10/10 | 25/11/10 | SKL 71 |
| 02/03/11 | PG 600 | " | 05/03/11 | 05/03/11 | N/A | |

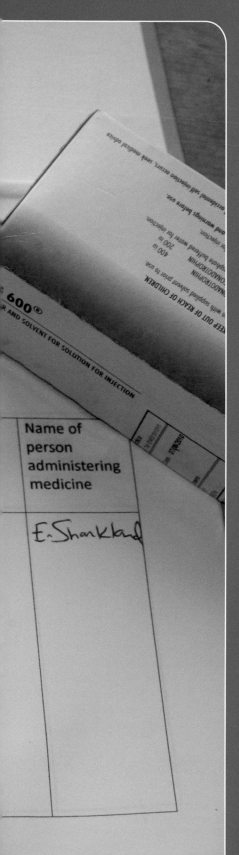

# LEGAL REQUIREMENTS

In the UK, there is no legal obligation to register your property as an agricultural holding. Your land may have been registered by the previous owner, but if it hasn't, the choice about whether to enter into the world of red tape is yours.

It all depends on your plans. If all you want to do is grow fruit and vegetables, keep a few chickens, maybe have some beehives, or even just turn your little bit of the world into a wildlife haven, there is no need to get involved in the bureaucracy that keeps the farming world in check. However, if you have more ambitious livestock-keeping plans – for instance, if you want to rear four-legged livestock – there are a few things you need to do.

www.roxan.co.uk

# How to register your property

### Step 1: Get your CPH number

The process of registering your holding is similar in England, Scotland and Wales, but varies slightly in Ireland (see Further information, page 172, for contact details).

In England, Scotland and Wales, you need a County Parish Holding (CPH) number, which identifies your land as a holding and allows you legally to keep four-legged livestock (you do not need it for poultry). The number will look something like this: 58/421/0086. The first two digits are the county, the next three the parish in which you live, and the final four the actual number of your holding. You will use this unique number whenever you buy or sell livestock, move animals on or off your premises, order identification tags and in various official documents.

Ireland does not use CPH numbers, but anyone wanting to keep livestock will need a herd and/or a flock number (see below).

Getting a CPH isn't difficult, doesn't cost anything, and shouldn't take too long. In England you will need to contact the Rural Payments Agency; in Wales, the appropriate divisional office of the Welsh Assembly Government; in Scotland, the Rural Payments and Inspections Department. Make a phone call and you will be sent some straightforward paperwork to complete and return.

### Step 2: Get a flock and/or herd number

Once you have the CPH, you will need to notify your local Animal Health and Veterinary Laboratories Agency (formerly Animal Health) that you are keeping – or intend to keep – livestock. You will be sent a herd or flock number to use if you move the animals to another location or to slaughter. This number will need to be imprinted on ear tags (or slap-marked) on any animal leaving your holding, whether going for slaughter, being sold to another holding, or travelling to a show or market.

In Northern Ireland, herd and flock numbers can be obtained from the Department of Agriculture and Rural Development, and in the Republic of Ireland, from the Department of Agriculture, Food and Marine.

### Step 3: Identification, tagging and movement records

Once you have your flock and/or herd number, you'll be able to order identification tags for your animals. Whichever company you choose will ask you for your CPH and your herd/flock numbers. (For information on identity and movement regulations for specific species, see the relevant section in Chapter 6.)

# Keeping veterinary records

If you keep livestock, you must maintain a record of any veterinary medicines administered. Records must be kept for three years and be available for inspection on request. If prescriptions are used as the record, they must be held for five years, and the dates of administration of the treatment must be related to the prescription.

Trading Standards departments will supply forms for you to complete and file, or you can store records on computer. The kind of details required include the date the medicine was purchased, its name, batch ID, and quantity purchased; the name and address of the supplier; the dates treatment started and finished; the date the withdrawal period ended; ID numbers of animals treated; the total quantity used; and the name of the person who administered the medicine.

# Transporting livestock

Everyone transporting livestock, whatever distance and whatever the total travelling time involved, has to ensure that certain welfare points are addressed:

- animals should be old enough and fit enough to travel
- journey times should be kept to a minimum
- those accompanying the animals should be sufficiently competent to look after them
- the vehicle and its loading and unloading facilities should be designed, constructed and maintained to avoid injury and suffering, and can be washed out and disinfected efficiently
- water, feed and rest should be given as necessary
- sufficient space should be provided
- animals of different ages, sizes and sexes should be grouped accordingly

## Transporter Authorisation

An EU regulation governing the welfare of animals during transport, which came into force in January 2007, requires that anyone transporting live vertebrate animals (i.e. those with a backbone) more than 65km (40 miles) in connection with an economic or commercial activity must apply for a Transporter Authorisation. This is granted by the Animal Health and Veterinary Laboratories Agency and must be renewed every five years.

The phrase 'economic activity' is not explained in the regulation, but the Department for Environment, Food and Rural Affairs (Defra) suggests it includes: 'Any transport of animals undertaken as part of a business or commercial activity, which aims at achieving financial gain, whether direct or indirect, for any person or company involved with transport.'

### THERE ARE SOME EXEMPTIONS, WHICH INCLUDE JOURNEYS:

- which are not in the course of business or trade
- which are not for hire or reward
- which involve a single animal accompanied by a person who has responsibility for its welfare (or two animals accompanied by two people, or four animals accompanied by four people – four is the maximum);
- which involve transporting an animal to or from a veterinary practice on veterinary advice
- where a pet animal is accompanied by its owner on a private journey

- where pet animals are taken to or from a specialist show or competition and the primary purpose is for pleasure rather than as part of a business
- where horses and ponies are transported by an owner for the purpose of riding, showing or competing for pleasure, e.g. show jumping, gymkhanas, etc. However, a haulier paid to take such animals to shows would require an Authorisation.
- where individuals attending shows or competitions primarily for pleasure share the cost of transport, but where there is no profit made by the individual undertaking the transport
- which are undertaken by the armed forces or public services during the course of their official duties
- which involve the transportation of circus animals where the transport vehicle is regarded as the animals' housing.

### THERE ARE TWO KINDS OF AUTHORISATION:

**Type 1** is for short journeys (more than 65km/40 miles and up to eight hours long);

**Type 2** is for longer journeys (more than eight hours).

For both types of journey, details of each journey must be recorded, preferably by completing an Animal Transport Certificate form (below), available from Animal Health, though information can be recorded in a home-made format. The information does not have to be sent anywhere, but must be kept on file for six months as part of the holding's movement records. The Animal Transport Certificate duplicates much of the information in the Animal Movement Licence (see Chapter 7 for more information).

## Certificate of Competence

In addition to the Transporter Authorisation, drivers and attendants accompanying vertebrates must have a Certificate of Competence. To obtain a certificate (and again, there are two types – one for short and one for longer journeys), you need to undergo an assessment at an approved examination centre, usually an agricultural college or another college of further or higher education. The assessment – which, at the time of writing costs between £50 and £60 – is aimed at testing your knowledge of animal welfare, particularly with regard to health and safety during transportation. You will have to answer a series of multiple-choice questions. The test can be carried out at your home for an additional fee.

You will need to take an assessment for each species you wish to transport, so if you plan to have several different animals and transport them relatively long distances, getting all the right bits of paper could be expensive.

## Trailer regulations

Animals have to be loaded, transported and offloaded in a safe and hygienic way. The obvious way is in a purpose-built livestock trailer or lorry, but many four-wheel drive vehicles can be fitted with livestock canopies that meet the various regulations.

Young stock may be transported in containers (such as dog crates or purpose-built boxes) and in a non-specialist vehicle, but the container and the space used for holding it must be suited to the purpose.

**ALL TRAILERS AND VEHICLES USED FOR TRANSPORTING LIVESTOCK MUST:**

- be well ventilated, so that excess heat and moisture can be removed
- be constructed in a way that prevents the animals from escaping or falling out
- have a non-slip flooring surface
- be capable of being thoroughly washed and disinfected at the end of the journey
- have lighting so that the animals can be inspected as necessary
- have suitable equipment to aid loading and unloading (such as a ramp and tail gates)

## Rules relating to ramps

There are specific EU regulations relating to ramps. They must not be steeper than an angle of 36.4% if you are transporting pigs, calves, or horses. For sheep and adult cattle, the angle should be no steeper than 50%. The best method of establishing the slope of your trailer ramp is to park it on flat ground with the trailer ramp down as shown in the illustration.

Measure the height of the trailer ramp as shown at point A, the ground length, marked B, and the tailgate length, C. The percentage slope is calculated by the height divided by the ground length and multiplied by the tailgate length.

In the example shown, the trailer height is 30cm, the ground length is 100cm and the tailgate length is 110cm – giving a slope of 33%. The calculation result is below the maximum of 50% and is therefore legal for the transportation of all animals. Modern trailers are designed to comply with these regulations. If you have an older-style trailer, it would be worth carrying out the calculation test to see whether it complies with the current rules.

Trailer angle calculation $\dfrac{A}{B} \times C$

**A** = Height
**B** = Ground length
**C** = Tailgate length

**Example**
**A** – Height = 30cm
**B** – Ground length = 100cm
**C** – Tailgate length = 110cm

Calculation $\dfrac{30}{100} \times 110 = 33\%$

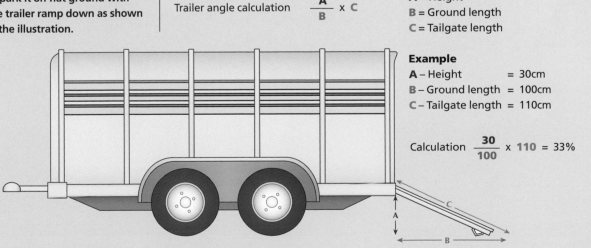

# ESSENTIAL KIT

A rotovator is a useful piece of kit, but larger areas of land will require bigger and stronger machines.

**It's impossible to give an exhaustive list of what you're going to need for your new lifestyle, because no two smallholdings are the same, and no two smallholders will have identical ideas or ambitions.**

Whatever the various features of the land and your personal requirements, it's safe to assume that you'll need to keep grass, scrub and hedges in check and, possibly, cultivate the ground. If you're the kind of person who is into "big boys' toys", you might be tempted to buy a host of expensive kit in your excitement – including the ultimate smallholder status symbol – the tractor. However, as with any purchase, it pays not to rush into things.

### Think before you buy

- Hire in help. You may find that it's cheaper to pay some-one to carry out an annual chore rather than splash out on a piece of seasonal machinery that may be used for a few days and then spend the rest of the year in the barn.
- Consider a tool or machinery swap. If your neighbour has something you need and he or she could do with borrowing something of yours, you might be able to come to an agreement.

Be careful what you buy, otherwise it could end up rusting away, unused.

- Machinery rings – organisations set up to help unite those who have with those who need – are becoming more and more widespread. The Machinery Ring Association of England and Wales supports 10 machinery rings in operation across England and Wales. It acts as a kind of 'broker', helping members hire out their equipment and skills to other members who need them. Ring membership is open to farmers, contractors, self-employed workers, mechanics, agricultural advisers, hire firms, and other businesses involved in farming activities (see Further information, page 172, for details).

## Safety first

Safety is of paramount importance when operating machinery of any kind. Unfortunately, as there are no restrictions on who can buy or use the potentially lethal equipment commonly found on a farm, and no requirements are in place for proper training to be carried out, numerous serious accidents – even deaths – are recorded year after year.

Before you contemplate handling an unfamiliar bit of kit – whether a power tool or a vehicle – get some formal instruction first. It will definitely be money well spent. Contact your nearest agricultural college or a farming union for advice on locating a course, and also take a look at the Health and Safety Executive's website for lots of useful information (see Further information, page 172). Don't forget to read any instruction manuals and to wear the correct personal protective equipment (PPE) before you try out any new purchase. Ensure that all equipment is well maintained – not just for reasons of efficiency, but also because a faulty machine can be a dangerous one.

This tree-feller didn't wear a safety harness and had a nasty fall just minutes after this picture was taken.

Hiring equipment can be risky if you don't know how to operate it. This mini-digger was overturned by an inexperienced user and had to be pulled out using a neighbour's tractor.

Ride-on mowers are fine for small areas, but go for the largest engine size, especially if you've got hills to drive up.

## Managing grassland

There are a few options here. Depending on how much land you need to keep in check, you may be able to cope with a ride-on mower, but if you have several acres to manage you'll need something with a bit more power under the bonnet. So what are the options?

### RIDE-ON MOWER

Designed for the domestic market, ride-on mowers are fine for anything between half an acre and 2 acres (0.2–0.8ha), as long as the land is fairly flat. Buy the most powerful machine you can afford, to minimise wear and tear. Bear in mind that, if your land is hilly, going uphill may be a struggle, hence the advice to go for a large engine size (about 14hp). Go for the maximum size cutting deck, too – normally about 107cm (42in) – because it'll save you a lot of mowing time. Some machines will allow you to tow small trailers or other attachments, up to about 772lb (350kg) in weight, but don't expect a mower to be too much of a multi-purpose workhorse.

### COMPACT TRACTOR

Modern, full-size tractors may look impressive and be essential on a large working farm, but most smallholders won't need anything that big and expensive.

The range of compact tractors – often called 'tractor mowers' – is growing all the time and, with a vast number being produced in Asia, they are increasingly affordable.

Many are supplied flat-packed and require self-assembly, but others can be assembled in advance for an additional fee. If you plan to construct it yourself, you'll need to be confident that you know what you're doing – or have the resources to pay someone to do the job for you – but it will help to keep down the overall cost.

Engine sizes range from around 15hp to 60hp, so this sort of tractor can be put to many different uses. Realistically, if you have more than 5 acres (2ha) to maintain, this is what you'll need. They are capable of pulling a flail mower or rotary topper, which attach to the three-point linkage system

Few smallholders will ever need a full-size tractor.

A tractor mower is a good compromise.

Restored tractors are often the pride and joy of their owners.

and are powered by the PTO (which stands for power take-off). The PTO will run a number of other labour-saving, implements, including rotovators, generators, balers, transport boxes, winches and hydraulic pumps.

Compact tractors have the advantage over full-sized machines in being lighter and easier to manoeuvre, and they also take up much less space when not in use. Along with regular maintenance, the other secret to longevity when it comes to machinery is to protect it, and being able to shelter your tractor from the elements whenever possible is an important consideration. A compact will fit into a large shed or an average-sized garage, even with an attachment like a front-loader or a topper attached.

### VINTAGE TRACTOR

There is something wistfully romantic about the traditional small farm tractor and there are plenty of people who would give their right arm to own a collectable David Brown or Massey Ferguson (the famous 'Fergie'). When you visit an agricultural show and see the rows of perfectly restored, highly polished veteran tractors on display, it's easy to ignore the fact that many machines of the same age are still being used as everyday workhorses. For every showroom-condition exhibit you will see, there will be hundreds more that are being put to work on farms across the land, day in, day out.

Restoring a classic tractor is so often a labour of love. The challenge of returning to working order something that may have been neglected for decades can be extremely

There is no reason why a veteran machine should not be both a thing of beauty and a working vehicle.

rewarding. But not all restorers are in the business of refurbishing a museum piece; for many, the aim is simply to get the tractor up and running as a working vehicle once again. This can often be a way of finding a relatively cheap and practical solution to a land management dilemma. There is a feeling among an increasing number of people that old tractors, cars and other vehicles, should be used and not just kept for special occasions. It is a bit like having an expensive piece of beautiful jewellery that is constantly locked away, never seeing the light of day or being enjoyed.

If you have the necessary maintenance skills and the dedication to restore an old tractor to its former glory, then go for it. You'll have the best of both worlds – reliability and aesthetic pleasure. It may cost you more in the long run, it may infuriate you at times, and it certainly won't have all the sophisticated mod cons of the latest machines, but, if you're the type of person who is prepared to give it a go, you'll love it.

Michele Baldock

An ATV is often top of the smallholder's list of must-have possessions.

## ALL-TERRAIN AND ROUGH-TERRAIN VEHICLES

All-terrain (ATV) and rough-terrain vehicles (RTV) are capable of carrying out a multitude of tasks on the smallholding or farm. They may have the reputation for being the ultimate farm plaything, but they are excellent and versatile workhorses and are often the smallholder's best friend.

First, let's look at ATVs. Often described as 'quads', they are single-cylinder machines that can be two- or four-wheel drive and are normally single-seaters, steered by handlebars similar to those on a motorcycle. As they are designed for just one person, they should never be used to carry passengers.

ATVs are loved by farmers because, driven correctly, they are 'go anywhere' vehicles and can reach areas that might be out of bounds for larger vehicles. Being so much lighter than conventional tractors, and even tractor-mowers, extremely muddy areas can be crossed and serious slopes can be tackled if the driver has the necessary skills.

More manoeuvrable and also more versatile than compact tractors in many respects, they come with a vast range of attachments, from harrows to muck spreaders. Mechanically, they are less complicated, too. There is no PTO, no three-point linkage, nor any hydraulics, and the engine is simpler, making maintenance more straightforward. All of which means that if you're not the DIY type, repairs should be cheaper, too.

Driving an ATV – once you have had the correct safety training – could not be easier. Most modern vehicles are automatic, so you can concentrate on manoeuvring, accelerating and braking. You'll also find that newer models have electric ignition systems, rather than the older kick-start or pull mechanisms.

ATVs can be modified for use on public roads, subject to the addition of various safety and identification features (such as indicators, lights and number plates) and registration with the relevant vehicle licensing organisation. This means you can run to the local agricultural supplier for feed or other supplies, or nip between blocks of your land that may be separated by public highways. They're particularly useful if you get snowed in and can't use other vehicles.

RTVs are the next step up in terms of versatility and comfort. Sometimes referred to as 'side-by-side' ATVs, because they have two seats rather than one, they are four-wheel drive vehicles and feature a load bay on the back, some of which can be tipped up. One of the great things about having a load bay is that it can save you the trouble of hitching up a trailer and, if your trailer-reversing skills leave much to be desired, backing into a small space is something that can be done with ease.

As with ATVs, most are automatic, leaving you to keep your mind on driving and safety. In any case, safety

RTVs (like those pictured above and below) are extremely versatile machines.

features on RTVs are far superior to those on ATVs. The big bonus is that the RTV is much more stable and less likely to tip over than the ATV. It also has a sturdy roll cage, so that, in the rare event of you turning one over, you'll be protected. In addition, there is a mesh panel behind the seats to protect both driver and passenger – so if you have a heavy load on the back and have to break unexpectedly, or if you are travelling down a steep hill, the cargo won't hit you in the back of the head. They also come complete with seat belts for both driver and passenger, plus handles to hold onto, should the going get tough. Like ATVs, RTVs can be registered for use on the road.

As you might have guessed, a good RTV will cost you a fair bit more than an ATV – probably about twice as much, but you have to weigh up the benefits against the additional expense.

Whatever you go for – simple ATV or the more useful RTV – make sure you buy something that has the power you need. If you are going to have to pull heavy loads, go for a bigger engine size. If you are aiming to use attachments, like a small topper or a harrow, something with an engine capacity of 250cc would be fine, but if you want to pull a larger trailer, maybe with a heavy load, you may be looking at something up to 400cc. If in doubt, consult the manufacturer for advice before buying.

# How to erect a stock fence

## What you need

**Get yourself some decent tools.**
**It would be useful to have:**

- chainsaw or bow saw
- claw hammer
- double shovels for removing stones and earth
- fencing pliers
- fencing staples and 15cm (6in) nails
- iron bar
- monkey strainer (or monkey puller), with straining ratchet and chain
- post knocker
- sledgehammer
- spades of various sizes
- straining bar
- tamping tool
- wire-twisting tool

**1** Dig a hole 20cm (8in) square and 46cm (18in) deep.

**2** Use double shovels to remove excess soil and stones.

**3** Bore a hole in the centre with the iron bar, so that the point of the post sits more comfortably. If digging a hole is difficult, consider either removing all the stone that's preventing you from digging further, or using concrete to infill around the stake you're about to insert.

**5** Measure the height the post needs to be, so you know how far to put it in. For a normal stock fence with a single row of barbed wire on the top, the height should be 120cm (47in) off the ground. For fences that require two strands of barbed wire on the top, the height needs to be 137cm (54in).

**4** Position a 2.4m (8ft) straining post in the hole and start securing it into place using a post knocker.

**6** The post will still be loose, so pack stones inside the hole to create extra stability.

**7** Use a tamper to compress the soil around the post.

**8** Look to see where you want your fence to end or turn. At the chosen point, install a second straining post, as before. As a general rule, strainers are used every 50m (55yd), or where there is a bend. In this example, the strainers are just a few metres apart, for illustration purposes.

**9** Tie some string between the two posts as a guideline, to help you position your other posts.

**10** Go back to your first strainer post and measure 66cm (26in) up the post from ground level.

**11** Position an intermediate post 1.8m (6ft) from the straining post. Secure the post into position using a manual post knocker.

**12** Dig around the base of the intermediate post and position the diagonal stay post in line with the 66cm (26in) mark measured earlier on the straining post.

**13** Trim off the end of the diagonal stay post so it's flush with the straining post. You can use a chainsaw or a bow saw for this job.

**14** Fit the stay post flush with the straining post, ready to be secured with 15cm (6in) nails.

**15** In order to prevent the post from splitting, blunt the sharp end of each nail with a hammer as shown.

**16** Fix the stay post to the straining post with a nail at a 45° angle.

**17** Insert a nail through the intermediate post into the straining post at ground level and at an angle.

**18** Take a roll of plain, medium gauge fencing wire.

**19** Make a loop in the end of the wire and twist to stop the loop from slipping.

**20** For the next part of the job it would be useful to have a specialist wire-twisting tool, obtainable from fencing suppliers.

**21** Use fencing pliers to hold the loop and use the twisting tool to tighten the loop.

**22** Fix the loop to the side of the straining post 2.5cm (1in) off the ground and secure with a staple.

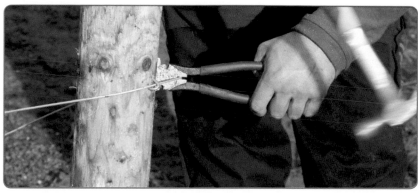

**23** Pull the wire around the intermediate post to the bottom of the strainer on the opposite side, fixing a staple half way along the stay post holder. Don't knock the staple all the way in at this stage, as you still have to tension the wire. As shown, use the fencing pliers to tension the wire around the intermediate post. Secure with a staple. At this stage, the staple in the stay post can be knocked in completely.

**24** Fix the wire 2.5cm (1in) above the ground on the opposite side of the straining post, using a staple. Again, don't knock the staple all the way in just yet.

**25** Using the fencing pliers, tension the wire and secure by knocking the staple in.

**26** Using the wire twister, secure the end of the wire to stop it slipping.

**27** Squeeze the two strands of wire running between the intermediate post and the stay post.

**28** Using the fencing pliers, twist the wires together several times to provide additional tension.

**29** You have now created a box strut. The box strut is the key to good fencing, as it provides a structure on which stock fencing is fixed and tensioned. There should be a box strut at 50m (55yd) intervals in a run of fencing, at 90° corners, and where the fence changes direction.

**30** Intermediate posts should be positioned at 1.8m (6ft) intervals between box struts.

**32** Using a monkey strainer, put the chain around the next straining post and loop it back through the eye of the tool to form a slip knot.

**31** It's now time to fix the fencing wire to the posts. The fencing wire should be on the side nearest to the animals in order to withstand the pressure when they lean or push against it. First secure the end of the stock fence to the straining post. Fix the fencing wire to the post with staples, starting at the bottom and working up. Place the staples at an angle to stop the wire slipping. On straining posts, use two staples per line, but alter the angle of the staples for better grip. The staples should be centred and all in line.

**33** Put the straining ratchet at the end of the chain.

**34** Attach the straining ratchet to the bottom strand of fence wire.

**35** Ratchet it up to take most of the tension.

**36** Get a straining bar.

**37** Using the straining bar, tension the fencing wire against the straining post. Position the wire as close as possible to the ground in order to stop stock pushing under.

**38** Put double staples in to secure the wire. Using the straining bar again, tension and secure the wire at the middle and top of the fence.

**39** Take a roll of barbed wire and fix one end to the first straining post. Use the width of a claw hammer as a guide to positioning the wire above the top of the fence.

**40** Move to the next straining post and mark the position of the barbed wire, again measuring with the claw hammer. Using the straining bar, tension the barbed wire as tight as possible and secure with a double staple. Secure the barbed wire to each intermediate post using the claw hammer again to ensure consistency.

A well-laid hedge is functional, attractive and provides food and shelter for wildlife.

Jonathan Stone

## Safety and security

Securing your boundaries is vitally important when you're planning to keep livestock. You need to make sure all your fences, hedges and walls are animal-proof – both to protect your own investments and to prevent any escapees damaging neighbouring property or causing road accidents.

Farming unions and numerous specialist firms offer combined insurance packages for the house, outbuildings, livestock and equipment, which normally include third-party liability. You should definitely take out insurance, but making sure that you minimise the risk of problems occurring is essential, too.

Replacing or repairing tired and broken fencing can be an expensive job if you want it done properly so you have a choice: pay someone to do the job or learn how to do it yourself. The following series of pictures show how the professionals set about doing the job.

## The value of hedges

Well-maintained hedges bring huge benefits to any farm or smallholding. Hedging is, of course, the cheapest and most natural form of barrier you can create, but it's so much more than that. Hedgerows are havens for wildlife, providing food and shelter for so many of our birds, mammals and insects. They provide green corridors along which small mammals like dormice can travel and link patches of crucial habitat together, just like stitches in a patchwork quilt.

Maintaining hedgerows is a labour-intensive job, but an extremely cost-effective one. Apart from buying a few tools, including an old billhook – which can be picked up at farmers' markets or car-boot sales for a few pounds – there's very little else to add to the cost. You may have to pay for a training course so that you can learn to do the job properly, but your investment will be a sound one, repaid many times over. Should you become sufficiently good at hedgelaying, you might even be able to hire yourself out to neighbours, making some money out of an enjoyable activity or bartering your skills with them for produce or help on your holding.

Making the first cut, which allows you to lay the stem, is probably the most crucial step.

As with all jobs involving tools, the correct clothing should be worn.

Lizzie Wilberforce

## Other useful bits of kit

### BRUSHCUTTER

This is absolutely invaluable if you have scrubland, particularly bramble-strewn areas that have to be hacked back before any serious removal work can take place. Not to be confused with a domestic strimmer used in suburban gardens, a brushcutter is a more heavyweight machine, capable of tackling considerably overgrown patches of land and of keeping working until the job is done.

The first major purchase for many smallholders is often a chainsaw, but a brushcutter is a much more important tool. Like the chainsaw, used in the wrong hands it can be extremely dangerous, so take advice on how to operate one, and try and get some formal instruction if at all possible.

Protective equipment must be worn. You'll need a helmet with a full-face visor because protecting the eyes and the rest of the face from small, sharp pieces of plant matter travelling at high speeds is essential. Gloves are not essential, but are worth having in order to protect the skin from sharp, flying chips. It is also possible to buy anti-vibration gloves, which are sufficiently padded to protect the hands from repetitive strain injuries, should the equipment be used for a long time.

Brushcutters can be fitted with a number of attachments to suit various jobs and, if a long blade attachment is being used, you should wear strong, protective boots. Shoulder harnesses will help support the weight of the brushcutter. A popular option is the single shoulder strap, but the full-body harness is the best choice, offering more padding over the shoulders. The additional comfort makes all the difference. Brushcutter blades should be examined carefully each time before use, as fractured blades can throw off potentially hazardous pieces of metal.

Used correctly, chainsaws can make short work of tough jobs.

### CHAINSAW

A chainsaw is an extremely handy bit of kit to have at your disposal, but it is also one of the most dangerous for the novice to handle. Before you start shopping around for one, get some proper training.

It is vitally important that you understand the safety guidelines involved and what protective clothing you need to wear. The Health and Safety Executive produces a free leaflet, *Chainsaws at Work*, which can be downloaded from its website (see Further information, page 172).

The gear, known as personal protective equipment (PPE), should conform to European safety standards. Your basic kit needs to consist of specialist chainsaw boots – or protective gaiters which fit over standard safety boots – chaps or trousers made of a fabric that can stop a moving chain if it comes into contact with them, chainsaw gloves and a safety helmet, complete with visor and ear defenders. Recommended, but not essential, is a protective jacket made of the same fabric as the specialist chaps and trousers.

It is a common mistake to think 'the bigger, the better', when it comes to buying a chainsaw. The secret is to buy something that suits your needs and which you can manage. The more comfortable it is to handle, the easier and safer it will be to use. Size is not everything: a saw with a 30cm (12in) side bar has the capacity to cut a log that is twice that diameter. For most of the time, the largest diameter logs you will need to deal with will be about 50cm (20in), so why buy something bigger which will make life more difficult for you and which you won't really need? Be realistic about your requirements and don't get something too heavy-duty or unwieldy – and potentially more dangerous.

Look for a well-balanced model that is light and easily lifted and has sufficient power to do the job you need. Check for features that will make it easy to use: ensure it's easy to start and that all the controls are straightforward and simple to reach. Find one with safety features built in that will stop the saw from operating, should it get caught in something. Specialist dealers will be happy to advise, so don't go shopping blindly in a general purpose store – go to someone who sells chainsaws on a regular basis.

Learn how to use a brushcutter before investing in one.

www.stihl.co.uk

# GROWING FRUIT AND VEGETABLES

If you're brave enough to take on a smallholding, you're probably pretty green-fingered and resourceful already, and you'll know exactly what you want to grow, why you want to grow it and how to get started. With that in mind, this chapter is an introduction to using your land to grow produce, and it assumes you already have many of the basic skills and some knowledge of the dos and don'ts of growing your own.

Before you start planting anything, the first thing to consider is the condition of your soil. Good plant growth depends on a healthy and efficient root system, and this means you must have reasonably good soil.

You may be fortunate in taking on a vegetable plot or garden that has been lovingly tended for many years. On the other hand, you may find yourself battling with a host of problems, which could range from heavy, compacted clay or waterlogged ground, to light, sandy soil almost devoid of any nutrients. You may hit huge boulders wherever you poke your fork, or you could have to battle with pernicious weeds like brambles, nettles, or dock before you can even get to the soil and see what you are dealing with.

Once all obstacles and hindrances have been removed, it's time to set to work on improving the soil. All soil types can be improved – though some may take more work than others. Organic matter – in the shape of well-rotted manure and compost – is an excellent soil conditioner that improves aeration and drainage. It can help drier soils retain moisture – and therefore reduce the likelihood of important nutrients leaching away – and it can equally improve the structure of very wet soil. And, of course, plenty of organic matter encourages the activity of earthworms, which help improve structure and aeration even further as they burrow and feed.

## Making compost

Making your own compost is an excellent way to dispose of waste garden and vegetable matter, but preparing it takes time and patience. For a compost bin to work efficiently, you have to create an environment in which the contents can rot down and decompose with the aid of bacteria. It needs air and moisture – but not too much so that it becomes wet – and insulation to

help retain the heat. A good, working compost heap can reach a temperature of 60°C (140°F) at its core, and this should help to kill off weed seeds and sterilise the compost.

Plastic bins can be bought from garden centres, and often from local authorities at subsidised prices, but it's relatively simple to build one of your own, using planks, wooden pallets, or off-cuts of wood. A piece of old carpet can be used as a cover, or you can make a wooden lid. A bin about 1m (3ft) square is a good size. Ideally, it should be sited in a sunny spot in order to make the most of the external heat in summer. It should also be put somewhere that's close to hand, to encourage you to top it up and mix the contents regularly and also monitor progress.

## What makes a good manure?

Manure is the obvious source of organic matter for most livestock keepers, but it should always be well rotted and, if taken from stabled animals, should not contain too much straw. As straw decomposes, it absorbs nitrogen from the manure, so the resulting product will not be as nutritious as it could be.

## The ideal compost mix

### What goes in

Unwanted fruit and vegetable peelings; manure; coffee grinds; tea bags; grass cuttings (though not in large quantities); straw; hay; crushed egg shells; garden prunings (chopped up small); weeds (don't include seeds if you can help it); paper (not glossy or coloured like magazines or leaflets); natural fibres such as cotton and wool.

### What stays out

Cooked food; meat; fish; bones; waste fat or oil; disposable nappies; invasive weeds such as nettles and Japanese knotweed; fireplace ash or coke; cat litter; diseased plants; large, woody branches. Try to avoid adding citrus fruits, evergreen plants and pine needles, which take a long time to break down.

A traditional slatted compost bin is easy to make from bits of spare wood. The front is removable so you can turn the contents.

## HOW TO START

1. Mix together sufficient material to create a layer about 15cm (6in) deep. If it's too dry, mix in some water.

2. Cover with a piece of carpet or a lid to retain heat and to keep out unwanted rain.

3. Add more ingredients regularly, making sure to finely chop anything which is tough, such as thick branches or stalks. Keep mixing to incorporate air, and keep checking for moisture.

4. Remember that the thicker the layer, the quicker it'll start to heat up.

5. Turning the contents every four to six weeks is essential to ensure that everything spends some time at the centre of the heap, where the temperature is hottest and decomposition occurs fastest. Turning also helps to promote aerobic activity; airless conditions encourage anaerobic bacteria, which cause purification. A bad smell will tell you that something is not quite right.

6. It is important to maintain the correct balance of carbon and nitrogen in the heap. Many older plants contain a great deal of carbon, and nitrogen is needed to allow micro-organisms to break it down. Activators like manure, or plants such as comfrey can be added to kick-start the process.

7. Depending on the type and size of the items you put in, your compost should be ready within three to six months, though it could take up to two years. Tough ingredients, such as straw and chunky branches, should be chopped up small and added gradually, mixing them with grass clippings, kitchen scraps and weeds which decompose at a faster rate.

8. Compost at the bottom of the bin will be ready first and so should be used first.

A plastic bin will do the job, but turning the contents will be trickier.

Ready-made compost is convenient, but can be expensive.

**Note: This chapter is not a complete guide to growing fruit and vegetables. You should refer to other literature and get advice. For comprehensive information on growing vegetables – see the Haynes *Home-Grown Vegetable Manual***

A polytunnel frame will last a long time, but the covering will need replacing at some point.

## Extending the growing season

Environmental conditions have a massive impact on the variety and quantity of produce you can grow. A greenhouse or a polytunnel can be a big investment, but a worthwhile one if you can manage it. Used ones often come up for sale in classified advertisements or on auction sites, so if you don't mind a bit of DIY, you could find yourself a bargain.

Like sheds, greenhouses and polytunnels do not normally require planning permission, but check with your own local authority, as interpretation of regulations varies.

Having the ability to grow plants from seed means you not only save money, but also get a head start on the growing season. It enables you to stagger your sowings, so that you have a succession of crops rather than ending up with one big glut. If you are considering selling your produce, continuity of supply is important. In addition, it allows you to grow crops which might be difficult or even impossible to be grown outdoors.

Growing from seed is both economical and extremely satisfying.

### LOCATING A GREENHOUSE OR POLYTUNNEL

There are some important factors to consider when siting your greenhouse or polytunnel. The more light that penetrates, the better, so avoid positioning it under trees or hedges; as well as restricting light, fallen leaves will encourage mould and lichens which, in turn, will have a detrimental shading effect.

Locating a polytunnel, in particular, should involve careful planning. To maximise use of sunlight, manufacturers normally suggest having the longest side of the structure running from east to west, as the sun will then travel from one end to the other. They also recommend choosing a sheltered site, to protect from strong winds, but that might not suit your particular smallholding. The good news is that most companies produce special base rails and storm-resistant braces that give extra stability. Some claim to withstand winds of more than 60mph.

## An orchard of your own

If you inherit an established orchard with your smallholding, take care of it. It is a sad fact that 60% of the UK's orchards had disappeared by the 1950s as land was turned over to other uses. In the post-Second World War years, farmers were paid handsomely for grubbing up orchards, as well as digging out hedges, draining ponds and hacking down ancient woodland, in the name of increased food production. Conservation organisations are warning that small traditional orchards could disappear altogether by the end of the century unless a concerted effort is made to save them.

Orchards became a major part of the landscape from Roman times and when our ancestors farmed they would always have a collection of fruit and nut trees near the homestead, which would have provided food for the family, produce to sell and shelter for livestock.

The relatively recent resurgence of interest in traditionally made cider and perry has stimulated enthusiasm for orchards. Individual projects to aid the care and restoration of existing orchards and to encourage landowners to plant new ones are taking place across the UK, but progress is slow. Contact your local authority to see if there are any schemes in place that may be of benefit to you, as some councils offer grants for new plantations.

Orchards are not just about producing apples for eating or cooking, or for making cider, perry, or wine. Often left ungrazed and unfertilised, they can be havens for wildlife, filled with wild flowers and grasses and providing a vital source of food and shelter. They play a key role in terms of conservation of numerous species, from insects and birds to small mammals.

Chickens grazing on pomace – the pulp left after crushing cider apples.

### PLANTING AN ORCHARD

Fruit trees do best on a sunny, sheltered site, where the ground does not become too waterlogged. The perfect site would be south-east to south-west facing, with shelter from the prevailing winds. The insects that pollinate fruit trees dislike gusty sites and may be discouraged from spending time in your orchard if the winds are too strong. Severe winds can also contribute to stunted growth and poor fruit yields. Most trees do best on well-drained soil, but if wet ground is a problem that cannot easily be solved, you could try building ridges or mounds and planting the trees on top.

Planting on a sloping site is a good idea to avoid blossom being killed off by late frost. Cold air is heavier than warm air and so finds its way into hollows, valleys and sheltered level ground. However, remember that the higher your site, the colder it will be.

### WHAT TO PLANT

Before you rush out and buy fruit trees, consider planting those which are best-suited to your area. If you can find them, old, local varieties will be suitable, as they will be well adapted and will have grown in similar conditions for generations. You'll also be doing your bit for conservation, helping to keep some of the rarer varieties in existence.

Specialist nurseries will normally offer a propagation service, grafting rare varieties onto suitable rootstock. The rootstock will have an impact on the ultimate size of the tree and its growth rate, and can also influence productivity, resistance to disease and general hardiness.

Cider making can grow from a hobby into a profitable business.

Another factor to bear in mind is pollination. Apple and pear trees are grouped according to when they flower and, therefore, when they can be pollinated. A specialist nursery will be able to advise on a good combination of trees to ensure pollination. Some fruit trees, including several types of plum, are self-fertile, requiring no additional help.

Generally, small trees will establish themselves far more quickly and effectively than older ones, and they will also be cheaper to buy. You will see them advertised as:

**Maidens or whips** Normally a year or two old and measuring up to 1m (3ft) high, the small size and flexibility means they will be more wind-resistant and more stable. The main disadvantage to buying this type of tree is that they will have been pruned less than an older tree before leaving the nursery, and so will have to be trimmed and trained into shape.

**Standards or half-standards** Two to four years old and larger than maidens, these will have been pruned repeatedly over the years and so have a good shape. The downside is that larger trees are more prone to wind rock and will need stronger staking.

## WHEN TO PLANT

**Bare-rooted trees** should be planted when they are dormant and not in leaf – any time between November and March in most parts of the UK.

**Pot-grown trees** can be planted at any time of the year, as long as there is no frost, but will need careful and regular watering. The roots should always be kept moist and cool before planting, whatever the weather.

## LAYING OUT YOUR ORCHARD

The most straightforward and practical way of creating an orchard is to create a square in which each tree is placed an equal distance from the next. The plan shown here has six trees across and five trees down, with a standard 10m (33ft) gap between each. This not only allows room for each tree to grow and develop, but also allows mowing machinery to be brought in to keep down the surrounding grass while the orchard is establishing, as well as harvesting equipment in future years.

As a rough guide, orchards of dessert and cider apple trees traditionally had a planting density of between 100 and 150 trees per hectare (about 50–75 trees per acre).

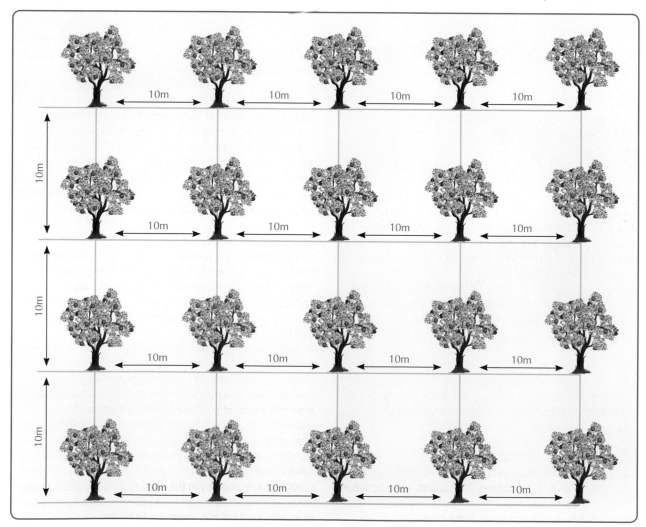

When fencing to protect trees, leave sufficient space so you can climb in to trim weeds.

## PLANTING YOUR TREES

- Young trees do not like competition from other vegetation, so clear all grass or scrub within a 1m (3ft) radius of the planting hole.
- Although maiden trees can be planted simply by making a notch in the ground with a spade, older, bigger specimens will need proper planting holes, sufficiently deep and with a wide circle to take their longer roots without constricting or bending them. When digging your hole, make sure you keep the topsoil and subsoil separate, and then return them to the hole later on in the correct order.
- Position a short stake in the hole, so that it stands about 30cm (1ft) above ground level. This will give support to the young tree and also allow it to bend and flex in the wind, thus strengthening the stem and root system.
- Insert the tree and backfill the soil around the roots until it's level with the root collar – the point at which it was previously planted. Water well, depending on the weather, and keep checking over the following few weeks to make sure it doesn't dry out.

## PROTECTING YOUR TREES

Animals, both wildlife and domesticated livestock, can be a challenge to newly planted trees. Tree guards – plastic tubes which can be wound around the base of trees – are effective against rabbits, which will gnaw at the bark.

Livestock pose a much greater threat, as they'll not only eat leaves and bark, but will also rub their heavy bodies against your trees, disrupting stability and snapping stems and trunks. Goats are particularly destructive, as they like to rear up on their hind legs to reach tasty leaves and often steady themselves by resting their front legs on upper boughs, snapping them in the process. The only answer is to keep all livestock out, or securely fence off each tree.

## ONGOING MANAGEMENT

You will need to learn how to prune your trees correctly. You could join a local organisation, such as a cider and perry society, orchard group, conservation body, or horticultural association, which would give advice. You'll find that groups such as these often offer discounted courses for members.

As well as keeping your trees in shape, you'll have to ensure that they don't have to compete for water and nutrients in the early years. It's important to keep a close check on weeds, ensuring that the 1m (3ft) circle you cleared around the base of the planting hole is kept free from unwanted vegetation, including grass, for at least three years after planting. This can be done by regularly applying a thick mulch, by strimming, applying a weed-suppressing mat, or by carefully using herbicides. In Victorian times, it was common practice to keep poultry in the orchard, to graze and scratch between the trees. So, if you can provide adequate predator-proof fencing, that, too, might be an option.

# YOUR FIRST LIVESTOCK

# GENERAL CONSIDERATIONS

When you have been dreaming of owning a smallholding for years and finally get the keys to your perfect place, it's extremely tempting to let your heart rule your head and rush into things, only to find that you have taken on too much too soon and live to regret it.

Impulse buys can be a big mistake, particularly when it comes to livestock. Just think how simple it would it be to buy some animals to fill those empty fields. Maybe you could have a few sheep or pigs, which would be easy on the eye when you gaze out of the window. And, of course, they would also eventually fill your freezer with wonderful, wholesome, free-range meat. But wait – have you thought of the practicalities? Ask yourself the following questions before you go too far along a route that may not be right for you.

## Do you need to keep livestock?

Is it really important that you raise your own meat? Maybe all you need is a way of keeping the grass down. It could be that you're thinking about having animals in your fields because of their aesthetic value. The fact is that you can do all of the above in other ways; you do not have to own

Good outbuildings are worth their weight in gold.

livestock. Unless you specifically want to raise your own animals for meat, you might be better off renting out your fields for grazing. That way your fields are kept in check, you get something nice to look at, but you don't have the expense of looking after them, nor responsibility for their day-to-day care.

## Do you have accommodation?

Have you got the land and buildings you'll need to keep livestock? Farm animals take up a lot of space, particularly if you have to rotate them between fields because of bad weather and constant poaching of the ground with heavy hooves. A common mistake is to underestimate how much land livestock needs, so take advice before making decisions.

You may want your animals to enjoy a free-range lifestyle, but shelter must be provided in case of extreme weather. You will also need a building which can be used to house sick or injured livestock, or for over-wintering, should conditions outside become too bad. Thinking further ahead, should you get into breeding you may want to bring the animals inside to give birth. You'll also need somewhere dry and safe from vermin to store feed and bedding.

## How secure are your boundaries?

Fences or hedges need to be sufficiently strong to keep your animals in and other people's out. You must ensure your livestock are kept safe, so do not skimp on fencing. You need to guard against your animals breaking out and damaging neighbours' land and property, or causing chaos on nearby highways.

## Insurance

Without doubt, you should obtain insurance to cover not only your livestock and buildings, but also third-party damage, just in case a break-out occurs.

## Do you have the skills you need?

Having the knowledge or experience to allow you to look after livestock is essential. You should be aware of what's likely to be required of you, and you must be prepared for all eventualities. Doing research and getting some training under your belt are top priorities.

## How good is your general health and strength?

Farming is an extremely physical lifestyle and not for the faint-hearted or the frail. Could you cope with the hard work involved, or do you have someone to rely on? Would you be up to wrestling with animals if you needed to restrain them?

Do you have a Plan B? You would need one. Consider what would happen if you fell ill or had an accident? Could someone in the family, or possibly a friend or neighbour, step into your shoes? Is there someone you could trust?

The hedge at the top has been neglected and would be no use at all. The picture below shows a denser stock-proof hedge.

You may be used to handling your livestock, but could you hand over the reins to a stand-in?

## What about medical emergencies?

Does the area have a veterinary practice and, if so, does it deal with livestock? More and more are turning solely to small animal work. Farm vets are like hens' teeth in some areas, so you may have to register with one some distance away. You will also need to have some rudimentary veterinary skills yourself. You will, for instance, need to administer injections and take temperature readings. Don't forget the old adage, 'Where there is livestock, there is dead stock.' At some point, you will have to deal with illness, injury and death.

## Preparation is key

As mentioned in Chapter 2, try to gain some practical experience with livestock before taking on any animals of your own. Whether you go for an organised training course, or arrange some informal shadowing with a neighbouring farmer, make sure you would be happy to carry out all the relevant husbandry duties on your own.

Most vets will insist on an introductory visit, so they know what they're likely to be dealing with in the future. They may suggest a health management plan involving a series of regular visits to coincide with routine procedures, such as worming and vaccination. Use your visits well. For instance, ask the vet to show you how to administer drugs or give vaccinations.

### The big question

**Could you kill an animal if you had to? There may be no one else around when the job needs to be done. Would you be up to it?**

Don't wait until your animals need help before registering with a vet.

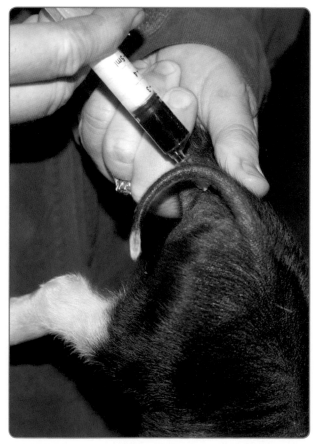

Smallholders learning about pig husbandry

A piglet being injected with iron

## The Five Freedoms

Being a responsible owner means granting your animals the Five Freedoms – a list of basic rights originally drawn up by the Farm Animal Welfare Council in the UK, but now internationally accepted:

**Freedom from hunger and thirst** Animals must have ready access to fresh water and a diet to maintain full health and vigour.

**Freedom from discomfort** They should have an appropriate environment, including shelter and a comfortable resting area.

**Freedom from pain, injury, or disease** Appropriate care should be given to prevent health problems, and there should be rapid diagnosis and treatment.

**Freedom to express normal behaviour** There should be sufficient space, proper facilities, and animals should have the company of others of the same species.

**Freedom from fear and distress** Mental suffering must be prevented by ensuring that animals live in appropriate conditions and are given appropriate treatment.

Pigs should be allowed to root – just one expression of normal behaviour!

## Buying your first livestock

Do your homework before making a purchase and buy healthy stock from reputable breeders. Good breeders sell good animals, free from disease or deformity, and won't take you for a ride because you're new to the game. A one-to-one transaction, carried out on a farm with good standards of biosecurity, rather than at a market filled with lots of other livestock, is also much less risky from a health point of view.

Word-of-mouth recommendations are worth their weight in gold. Ask around locally and find out who rears what. Alternatively, if you're interested in a particular breed, check out the breed society websites, which will normally have contact details for members.

You may find that when you agree to buy your smallholding, the vendor offers to sell you not just machinery and equipment that could be useful, but some or all of the resident livestock. Unless you're ready to take the plunge, don't. It could be too much too soon. Also, how would you know if what you were buying was fit and healthy, or worth the asking price? Don't necessarily think you'll be getting a bargain; most animals are fairly cheap to buy, so don't be rushed into becoming a livestock-keeper before you are good and ready.

## Buying at auction

Another thing to be wary of until you have got a bit of experience under your belt is buying at auction. Auctions are great fun and extremely exciting, but are riddled with pitfalls for the novice buyer. Would you know how to tell the age of a sheep? Could you tell if a sow's udder would support a full

*Auctions can be tempting, so make sure you really want something before bidding.*

litter? Do you know foot rot when you see or smell it? Could you carry out the necessary health checks amid the hustle and bustle of a market?

Keeping your hand in your pocket can be difficult when you're caught up in the atmosphere of a busy sale, and there is the possibility of getting carried away and bidding on something you don't really need. Similarly, it's easy to get locked in a bidding war with another novice, which pushes the price up to an unrealistic level.

Having said all that, auctions are brilliant entertainment, and there is nothing like going home, safe in the knowledge that you've snapped up a real bargain – even if it's stinking out the back of the vehicle and creating a deafening racket.

So, if you're going to take a gamble at an auction, there are a few things you should bear in mind:

1. At first, go as a visitor rather than a buyer. Learn about the way auctions work – find out how to register and get your bidder's number; how much commission and VAT you will have to pay; the methods of payment accepted; when you can collect your purchases.
2. Work out what equipment/vehicle you will need to transport your animals home. For instance, poultry breeders tend to bring their birds in cages or crates, which they take home with them, so you will not necessarily be given a cardboard box for your chickens. Driving with birds or other livestock loose in the back of your vehicle is neither safe nor pleasant.

Remember the old adage: 'buyer beware' when at an auction.

3. If you know an auction is coming up, contact the organisers for a copy of the catalogue. This will give you time to see what is on offer, do some research into breeds and check the current market prices, so you don't bid over the odds.

4. Take someone knowledgeable with you. You can't beat the advice of someone who has experience of buying and rearing the type of animals you've set your sights on.

5. Arrive early and note down which lots interest you. Give yourself plenty of time to have a good look at the livestock and make sure it's what you really want to buy. If you turn up when the auction is about to start, you will be straining your neck to see what's being sold. Also, you will need to register and collect your buyer's number before you can start bidding.

6. Check how many animals are being sold in each lot. In poultry auctions, for instance, the auctioneer may offer six birds for sale, but the bidding will be for a single bird rather than the entire half dozen. If you win, you'll have the option of buying some or all of the birds at the winning price. Listen closely to what the auctioneer says before bidding starts.

7. When you're taking a look at an animal before the auction, make sure it's fit and healthy. Never buy anything that looks too quiet, or generally under the weather, thinking it will be much better when you get it home. Basic things to watch for include:

- General appearance and posture – listlessness, dull eyes, droopy head, dry muzzle, reluctance to stand
- Discharge from eyes or nose; scouring (i.e. diarrhoea)
- Generally poor coat/skin – dull or scruffy hair or feathers, bald spots, scabs; animal scratching a lot
- Coughing or sneezing – could indicate respiratory problems
- Lameness or other signs suggesting the animal is in pain
- Lumps in udders, suggesting mastitis
- Poor or missing teeth, which could cause feeding problems

8. Make sure in advance that you have accommodation ready for whatever you buy. You do not want to have to keep animals cooped up for hours in a vehicle or trailer while you prepare their new home.

# THE LIVESTOCK

This section is not intended to be an exhaustive guide to choosing and caring for all manner of livestock, but more an introduction to the kind of animals you might consider keeping on your smallholding. It doesn't venture into breeding because mastering the business of looking after livestock – a tough enough task in itself – should always be the first step.

Work towards learning the basics of animal husbandry and gaining a thorough understanding of the health and welfare needs of your chosen species before moving on to breeding. See Further Information, page 172, for a list of recommended publications – including other Haynes Manuals – plus contacts for relevant clubs, breed societies, and other organisations.

# KEEPING BIRDS

## Avian influenza

International outbreaks of avian flu in recent years changed the rules and regulations regarding keeping poultry and other birds in the UK. Although there is still no requirement for poultry-keepers to have a County Parish Holding number (see Chapter 3), anyone with more than 50 birds must now supply their details to the Great Britain Poultry Register. This applies even if your birds only reach 50 at certain times of the year, for instance, if you rear turkeys for the Christmas or Easter market. Those with smaller flocks don't have to register, but are encouraged to so that if an outbreak occurs they can be given early warning and advice.

The birds covered by the register are chickens, ducks, geese, turkeys, partridges, guinea fowl, quail, pigeons, pheasants, emus, rheas and ostriches.

Poultry keepers are not bound by the movement rules that apply to those who farm other animals. You can buy or sell a bird without having to fill in any official movement documents and without informing your local trading standards department.

Few people who keep poultry are complacent about the risks posed by avian flu, but they have to be kept in perspective. In order to be infected, you first need to be suffering from human flu (and not just a cold or the sniffles),

*Learn to understand what is normal behaviour, and watch for changes.*

and you have to be in extremely close contact with an affected bird – closer than most poultry keepers would ever get. Avian flu cannot be caught from eating eggs or poultry meat. You would have to ingest faeces, saliva, or mucus from a bird at the infectious stage. Eating eggs and properly cooked poultry meat poses no threat.

Certain birds, including swans, Muscovy ducks and geese, are regarded as sentinel birds with no resistance to avian flu, and are therefore early indicators of problems. More than one death should be reported.

Dead birds should be carefully bagged, and care taken to avoid contact. Hands and clothes that come into contact with the carcasses should be thoroughly washed as soon as possible.

Although the risk of avian influenza is low, birds can carry other respiratory infections. They can also transmit infections that can cause gastrointestinal illnesses. The advice is to
- practise good husbandry
- be observant
- know your birds
- act quickly and correctly should you spot anything unusual.

## Protecting your stock from predators

Don't underestimate the cleverness and determination of foxes, badgers and other predators. Your birds must be kept in a safe run or enclosure, otherwise, sooner or later, you will have an unpleasant surprise. Most foxes patrol their territory at all times of the day, and the increasing trend for well-meaning folk to feed them in their back gardens in towns and cities means that modern-day foxes are far less afraid of humans and much more opportunistic.

Electrified tape surrounds this wire poultry fence for extra security.

Predators are more likely to dig under a fence than try to climb over it. A standard 120cm (4ft) high fence can be made more fox-proof by attaching a kind of skirt – a small-gauge fencing wire – to the bottom, then burying it under stones and earth. Eventually, grass grows through the wire and knits it tightly into place. When a fox or badger approaches the edge of the fence and starts digging, the buried wire gets in the way.

Electric fencing can also be used around the perimeter fence, but make sure that, if it's powered by a battery, you check regularly to make sure it's still working. Wet grass can cause the fence to short, so strim regularly.

Other, rather more bizarre methods of deterring predators are recommended by some. These range from scattering human hair clippings around the fence to urinating to mark the territory, just as a fox or a dog would. Llamas and alpacas are supposedly good guardians of flocks because they instinctively defend their companions.

If all else fails, you may find you have to invest in a specialist trap or hire someone experienced in shooting predators. It may be a difficult decision to make, but you have to weigh up the moral argument against how much you could lose, and the suffering that could be caused to your flock.

One of the most annoying things about foxes is that they kill indiscriminately. Their initial aim might be to source food for themselves or their cubs, but a primeval instinct tells them that, once they have gained access to a pen, they need to kill everything in sight.

## Wing-clipping

It is all very well stopping predators from getting in, but if a bird insists on getting out, it is likely to become a takeaway meal. Unless you want to build a prison-height fence, wing-clipping is the answer. This involves snipping off the flight – or primary – feathers of one wing. Only one wing is clipped so that it unbalances the bird, making flying impossible. Ask someone with experience to show you how it is done, or ask your vet for advice if you do not feel sufficiently confident.

Clipping is a painless procedure – a bit like trimming nails – but you have to be careful not to cut too far up the quill of the feather or you will draw blood. If this happens, separate the bird from the others for a few minutes, until the bleeding stops. Clean away any blood before returning it to the flock, otherwise it might be attacked.

Make sure you trim only the primary feathers, the others are for insulation. You'll have to repeat the process once a year, as some of the cut feathers may be moulted out and replaced by new ones. Be careful not to cut new feathers that emerge after moulting, because they will bleed.

# Chickens

Ask most newcomers to smallholding what is at the top of the shopping list, and 99% will say chickens. They are easy to keep, demand only basic animal husbandry skills, and they are also entertaining and rewarding. Once settled in, they will give you far better eggs than any you will buy in a supermarket, and all you have to do in return is provide food, water and a safe, hygienic and dry place for them to live.

You might consider raising chickens from day-old chicks, or even eggs, as a cheap way of starting a flock. However, this does require some skill, time and specialist brooding equipment, and mortality rates can be disappointingly high. Beginners are better off buying young hens that are about to start producing eggs. These are known as point-of-lay pullets, and are normally about 18–20 weeks old.

Before you go too far, check that the deeds of your property do not include a clause which forbids you from keeping chickens or other animals.

**For a complete guide to keeping and breeding chickens, see the Haynes *Chicken Manual* by Laurence Beeken (Haynes Publishing).**

## Choosing breeds

The type of birds you choose will depend largely on whether you want them solely as layers, or to double up as table birds, too. Some birds are regarded as dual purpose because they're heavier, meatier breeds. The number of eggs you expect is important; commercial hybrids are superior layers – some producing up to 300 eggs a year – whereas pure breeds will be far less productive and will be more likely to go broody.

Ex-battery hens are often a popular choice with first-time chicken keepers. Commercial units sell off their birds between the ages of about 10 months and two years old

Hens rescued from battery farms soon perk up and adapt to outdoor life.

and replace them with new stock. The unwanted birds are commonly sold to meat processing plants or pet food manufacturers, but lots of animal rescue organisations specialising in poultry collect birds on a regular basis and rehome them. Hens that have been kept indoors in intensive conditions may look a little rough and take a while to get used to a free-range lifestyle, but giving a good home to a bird that might otherwise have ended up in a chicken pie can be very rewarding.

Appearance is an influential factor when choosing any type of livestock. Everyone's preferences differ and there are hundreds of breeds available. Getting to see the sheer variety of birds on offer is always a good idea. Specialist poultry shows and sales provide the ideal opportunity to view different types and to talk to breeders.

Most of the popular breeds have bantam varieties – miniature versions – so if space is an issue, these could be the answer. They lay smaller eggs, but eat less and so cost less to keep. Easier to handle, they are a good choice if children are to be involved in the rearing process. Be warned, bantams tend to get broody more often than standard-sized birds, so make sure you collect the eggs several times a day to stop any maternal feelings developing.

A mixed flock of birds is an attractive sight, and picking up a basket of differently coloured eggs is always rewarding. However, if you want to mix breeds, reduce the risk of fighting by buying them in at the same time and by choosing birds of similar sizes. Introduce them all simultaneously rather than trying to integrate some at a later stage. Also, put them into their coop together when it is dark, so they can't see who's who.

## Popular choices

**Araucana** These lay the coveted blue-green eggs favoured by supermarkets at the higher end of the scale. The blue gene is dominant, so is carried on even if the birds are cross-bred. Araucanas are fairly small birds, but can be raised for meat. They come in various colours, with the most popular shade being lavender – a soft silvery-grey.

A mixed flock is a popular choice.

**Black Rock** A hardy, good-laying hybrid, created by crossing a Rhode Island Red with a Barred Plymouth Rock (female line). Docile and easy to handle, it has thick plumage – either black with a green sheen or black and golden brown – and lays medium brown eggs for a surprising length of time, sometimes as long as 10 years.

**Marans** The French Marans is a favourite with many because of its ability to supply both eggs and meat, but also because it produces chocolate-brown eggs in good quantities. The most common variety is the Cuckoo Marans, with black and white speckled plumage.

**Buff Orpington** The Golden Retriever of the chicken world, it has handsome, dense, strawberry-blond plumage and lays brown eggs. An extremely attractive addition to any flock, and even lovelier free-ranging in a garden setting.

**Light Sussex** One of the oldest breeds in the UK, this large bird is easily recognisable with its white body, black 'cloak' of shoulder feathers, and black tail. Suitable for both eggs and meat, it's a good bet for all climates.

**Rhode Island Red** One of the most popular of all breeds, favoured for both its eggs and meaty shape, this American bird is one of the best of the dual-purpose breeds. A hardy breed with deep reddish-brown feathers, it's used extensively in producing hybrid varieties.

**Welsummer** The male of this Dutch breed is the archetypal handsome farmyard cockerel – the sort you see immortalised in ornaments and on a certain brand of cereal. The hens are attractive, too, with brown plumage that changes from gold at the neck to dark brown at the tail. They lay large, dark-brown eggs.

## First hens

Buying point-of-lay hens from a good breeder is by far the easiest way to start off. When you get your hens home, give them time to settle. It's worth shutting them into the coop for the night and part of the next day, so they grow accustomed to their new surroundings. Provide food and water inside until they are ready to brave the great outdoors, which will not be long.

The size of coop your birds will require will vary, depending on how big they are and how many you have. But, as a general rule of thumb, each bird needs about 20cm (8in) of perch space, with the lowest perch about 60cm (2ft) off the ground. If you're buying a purpose-built house, it may have ready-made nest boxes, so sleeping and laying areas are kept separate, meaning less chance of dirty or broken eggs. You can always adapt a large rabbit hutch or a garden tool shed into a suitable home, making sure there is sufficient ventilation and providing boxes for laying. The Haynes *Chicken Manual* contains a step-by-step guide to building a straightforward hen house that can be adapted to suit your needs.

Bedding inside the house is a matter of choice. Most people opt for straw, but others prefer wood shavings or shredded newspapers. Some install slatted bases to the coops so droppings fall straight through, though most purpose-built modern houses will have solid floors.

Feeding chickens is straightforward. Good-quality layers' pellets are widely available and offer a carefully balanced diet designed for optimum growth and egg production. You can buy your own ingredients and blend your own feed, but you need to have a good grasp of what you're doing in order to ensure you provide the correct nutrition.

- Don't feed your birds more than they can clear in five minutes, or you will just be feeding the local wildlife and vermin.
- Don't forget the importance of water. You will be surprised how much chickens drink.

## Health

Most poultry-keepers with small, free-range flocks will never have any problem with serious infectious diseases. If you buy your chickens from a good breeder, they will probably have been vaccinated against the most commonly seen problems, which include Marek's disease, Newcastle disease and infectious bronchitis. Birds from big commercial operations will most probably have been tested for salmonella, too.

Good husbandry is the key to keeping your birds healthy, so regular cleaning and disinfecting of chicken houses is a must. This minimises the risk of respiratory diseases spreading and, when combined with regular dusting using an appropriate insecticide, lessens the risk of external parasites.

The most common problems you are likely to encounter include scaly leg (caused by a small parasite burrowing under the scales), mites and lice, and internal worms. All of these conditions are treatable if spotted sufficiently early, so inspect your flock regularly and stay vigilant.

## Should you keep a cockerel?

A misleading old wives' tale says that hens lay better in the presence of a male. Unless you want to start breeding, or would like meat for the table, there is no point in keeping a cockerel; it will be more trouble than it's worth. Cockerels are sex machines, pestering the hens mercilessly. They rip out feathers and tear skin in the heat of mating, and can cause so much stress that the hens lay less. They can be aggressive to their owners, too. Chances are, your near neighbours will not be too keen on them, either.

# Ducks

Ducks are often a natural progression after chickens but, entertaining as they are, they are very different creatures and can be a controversial purchase because of potential disturbance to neighbours. Call ducks, with their repetitive cries, have sparked numerous disputes. Think carefully before investing in something that could cause a serious falling out and talk to your neighbours about your plans.

Also, if you are a keen gardener, be warned that they can be destructive when it comes to anything green, devouring all vegetation in sight and leaving nothing but a muddy mess.

So that's the bad news. The good news is that ducks can, indeed, be delightful creatures. Often more attractive and engaging than chickens, they are also a lot less demanding in terms of day-to-day care. They are not fussy eaters, surviving quite contentedly on standard chicken feed, and they do not suffer from as many ailments as hens. Many breeds are prolific layers, producing far more eggs than hens, and they can be a big help in the garden, eating slugs and snails – though you might have to sacrifice a few plants.

## Ducklings or adults?

It is easy to be tempted by ducklings. They are undeniably cute, they are cheap and you will tame them much more easily than older birds.

But, as always, there are drawbacks. The first thing you need to know is that if you are offered a box of motherless, fluffy ducklings, you will have to keep them under a brooder lamp (an infra-red light, which is suspended above the birds to keep them warm) until they develop their first feathers. Before they're completely feathered, duckings that have been raised artificially should not be allowed access to a pond, because they won't be waterproof. The preen gland, found at the base of the tail, secretes an oil which the bird spreads, using its beak, onto its feathers and claws. In the natural world, a duck will preen her young until they can manage by themselves, giving them the all-important waterproofing. Incubator ducklings, however, have to learn to do it themselves, so the process takes longer.

Like chickens, it's best to start by buying birds at point of lay. In ducks, this means approaching 24 weeks. Sexing adult ducks is straightforward, whereas ducklings can be easily confused. With adult birds, the calls are very different. Females give a characteristic 'quack', while the call of the male is a more rasping or scraping sound. Appearances are also quite distinct, too, with males tending to have more showy and colourful plumage. The tail can be a give-away, with drakes developing inward-curling feathers on the rump from the age of 14 weeks. The advantage of buying from a good breeder is that the stock will already have been sexed, and you can specify what you want, so you won't end up with too many drakes.

## Ducks and water

Ducks need access to water, but you do not have to have a pond. Obviously, a pond is a more natural environment, but unless it's fed by a spring, it'll soon get dirty. Ducks need to be able to wash and preen, but they can do this in a container such as a children's paddling pool or an old bath. It is important to provide something deep enough for them to completely submerge their heads so that they can splash water over their bodies, but heavy enough so that it cannot tip over. A container will need to be cleaned out and refilled every day, because stagnant water can pose health problems, but a container could be the solution if you can't have or don't want a pond.

Preening is important to both ducks and geese because it helps to protect the feathers from waterlogging. The preen gland on the rump at the base of the tail produces fatty and waxy substances that are released when the bird stimulates it with its beak. If preening isn't carried out on a regular basis, or if the bird can't clean its feathers and they become coated in dirt and mud, a condition called 'wet feather' can occur. The appearance of the feathers changes, so they look damp instead of glossy, and they lose their water-resisting capabilities. The bird becomes cold and miserable and avoids water, which can lead to other health problems.

## Accommodation

Ready-made duck houses aren't seen as regularly as chicken houses, but you should be able to find a supplier by checking the specialist smallholder magazines. It's easy to modify an existing chicken shed or rabbit house to suit.

As a general rule, large breeds should have around 0.19sq m (2sq ft) of space inside, and the internal height of the house should be about 90cm (3ft). If you're adapting a chicken house, take out the perch (ducks and geese do not roost like hens) and block up the pop-hole, which will be too small to use.

The drawback of adapting a hen house is that you have to shut the ducks in at night and let them out after they've laid early next morning. Ducks are not like hens, returning to their house to lay their eggs. If they are allowed to come and go as they please, they will start laying all over the place – even in water.

## Health

Ducks are hardier than chickens, as long as you remember the key things: food, clean water and clean, hygienic surroundings.

**Lameness** Often it's just muscle strain caused by getting in and out of the water awkwardly but it can also be a sign of infection that would require treatment.

**Parasites** Like chickens, ducks can pick up internal parasites from wild birds, but treatments are widely available.

**Botulism** One of the most serious conditions affecting waterfowl is botulism, a killer caused by a bacterium found in stagnant water. The secret lies in prevention – keeping ponds and water containers free of dirty water.

---

### Ducks and drakes: how many?

The simple answer is, if you don't want to breed from your ducks, don't bother with a drake. Just as you don't need a cockerel to get your hens to lay eggs, you don't need a drake to get your ducks in the mood, either. Ducks are often sold as trios – one drake and two ducks – but a ratio of one to seven is kinder. Drakes are rough and voracious lovers. By increasing the size of the harem, the 'workload' is shared more reasonably.

## Choosing breeds

All but one of today's popular breeds are descended from the wild mallard. The exception is the Muscovy, which originated from Central and South America. Mallards are thought to have been domesticated in Egyptian times and, until Victorian times, ducks were kept primarily for meat rather than eggs. Today, many people – particularly keen bakers – prize the bigger, richer duck eggs far above those of hens.

Everyone has their personal preferences, but here are some of the most popular:

**Aylesbury** Originally called the White English, this large, white bird gets its name from the Vale of Aylesbury. It's fast growing, so economical to keep if you're raising for meat. There are lots of commercial white hybrids which are Aylesbury 'lookalikes'.

**Call Ducks** Probably the least destructive of all ducks, because of their small size and habits. They come in lots of different colours and varieties, so there is sure to be one to suit your tastes. However, be warned that their repetitive calls – used by hunters to lure in wild ducks – can prove irritating.

**Indian Runner** These are the 'wine bottles' of the duck world – thin and upright, with long necks. If you have visited a big agricultural show, you may have seen a shepherd who trains runners to behave like sheep. Runners are excellent layers, but too skinny for meat.

**Khaki Campbell** This reliable layer is one of the most popular choices for commercial egg producers. Created by crossing the Indian runner, mallard and Rouen, it's a small brown-feathered bird producing white eggs on an astonishingly regular basis.

**Muscovy** With the bright red 'mask' around the eyes and on top of the beak, this is a duck you'll either love or hate. They are big, strong birds, and their feet have claws – which help them climb trees – so they need to be handled with care. They do not swim a lot, because their oil glands are not as efficient as other ducks.

**Rouen** This French breed looks similar to the wild mallard but is much bigger – often reaching 5.4kg (12lb). Although its size would suggest it would be good as a table bird, it grows slowly, so it is not popular with commercial breeders. Egg laying is poor, too.

**Silver Appleyard** A great dual-purpose breed, it is a good layer and an excellent table bird; it looks good, too, with a mallard-like green head and silvery-grey and fawn feathers elsewhere. There is a miniature version of the breed as well.

# Geese

Geese have stronger and more distinct personalities than any other domesticated birds. They are very communicative and form strong bonds with humans, making them rewarding pets. They are also adept at keeping the grass down and clearing weeds, slugs and snails, and they make good house alarms, too. There is a growing demand for geese for the table, particularly as an alternative to the usual festive roast. They are certainly back in fashion – a fact borne out by the phenomenal price per kilo when compared with other meat birds.

Research carried out for the rural and environmental consultancy ADAS revealed that goose meat was better for us than experts previously thought. Studies showed that the meat had a lower fat content than either lamb or beef. In addition, the fat contained a relatively low proportion of the 'bad' saturated fats, but a higher proportion of the 'good' mono-unsaturated and essential fatty acids.

The eggs are much larger than those of hens and ducks. Although they're less popular for everyday use, they're considered good in cakes and pastries.

Waterfowl make greater demands on land than hens, and geese, in particular, need to graze. If kept in too small a space, they will soon wreck the ground. As a general rule, 0.4ha (1 acre) of grassland can support about 40 to 50 geese. However, it is advisable not to over-graze the same area, otherwise there can be a build-up of gizzard worm.

Free-draining soil is good, as is an orchard, but any ground with grass and other vegetation will do. Although they prefer good, young grass, geese will also do well on rougher areas of land. However, grass must be kept short – no taller than 10cm (4in). Short grass provides greater nutrition, while longer, tougher grass can get stuck in the crop, with fatal results.

One potential solution is to keep geese alongside cattle or sheep, which will eat the tougher stuff, leaving the new growth for the geese. Some supplementary feeding is normally recommended – a mixture of chicken pellets and wheat is a popular choice.

## Accommodation

Geese do not need anything special, just shelter from the sun and rain, so you could use an open-fronted pole barn or a shed adapted to give added ventilation. They'll make a mess of their sleeping quarters, so a thin layer of wood shavings or sawdust should be used to keep the floor dry and soak up droppings.

The shelter should ideally have nest boxes on the floor of the house. These can be purpose-built or made out of the kind of wooden crates you find in a greengrocer's shop. Like ducks, geese do not roost, so you won't need perches.

Geese will always enjoy a pond, but it is not essential to provide one, they just need good access to water. They must be able to wash themselves and preen, and containers can be provided to fulfil this need, as long as they are cleaned out on a regular basis.

## Behaviour and good relations

The tolerance levels of your neighbours should be a consideration when deciding whether or not to raise geese. Ducks may be noisy, but geese win the contest hands down every time, so make sure that those who live nearest to you are prepared for what you're thinking of inflicting on them.

Geese can be aggressive. Some breeds, particularly Chinese geese – which are descended from the wild swan goose – have a reputation for being boisterous. As with all animals, socialisation from an early age will help encourage a better temperament. Birds which are well handled from the point of hatching can be a pleasure to have around, but if you buy older birds from a place where they have had little human contact, they will inevitably behave differently. Whatever breed you choose, children should not be left with them unsupervised, particularly during the mating season. Similarly, if you have young children with small pets, be warned that geese are omnivorous and will eat anything from slugs, snails and worms, to mice, baby rats and even hamsters.

## Choosing breeds

Your choice of bird will be largely determined by the reason for keeping geese – whether for meat, eggs, or as pets. Good laying birds will produce about 60 eggs a year – with each egg the equivalent in size to about three hen's eggs.

Geese fall into three groups: light (4.5–8kg/10–18lb), medium (6.5–9kg/14–20lb) and heavy (9–16kg/20–35lb). Ganders are naturally heavier in all breeds. Here's a selection of some of the most popular breeds:

### LIGHT GEESE
**Pilgrim** If Chinese geese are the rogues of the species, Pilgrims are the angels, much prized for their gentle temperament. Originally from Britain, the bird was taken to the United States by the Pilgrim Fathers. The goslings can be sexed on hatching, because of the colour of the down and bill. Adult males are mainly white with some grey; females are light grey, with white feathers at the front of the head.

**Roman** Imported to other parts of Europe at the turn of the 19th century, these are short, stocky, mainly white birds, which are easily recognised by their short necks and small body length. They are popular as a meat bird and are a good breeder.

**Sebastopol** The origins of the Sebastopol are unclear, though the name suggests it came from the Crimea. This is the pantomime goose, with its long, curly white feathers, and a breed in great demand. Most birds are white, but a buff variety also exists. There are two variations in plumage: the frizzle, which has curly feathers all over the body, but not on the head and neck, and the smooth-breasted.

*The Sebastopol's flamboyant feathers make it extremely sought-after*

Embdens are good for both meat and eggs.

The broad-chested Pomeranian.

## MEDIUM GEESE

**Brecon Buff** A Welsh breed, very popular for meat, eggs, and showing. It has buff and white plumage with a pink beak and feet. Hardy, and used to the wet Welsh climate, it needs access to water more than some breeds, and also prefers to forage rather than be kept in a yard. Considered a fairly placid breed, and it doesn't fly a lot. Good for beginners.

**Pomeranian** A German breed descended from the European greylag, colours include grey and white saddleback. Broad-chested, following decades of careful breeding for meat, it has a distinctive, bold head, and an orange-pink bill. The heavy breast makes the birds look horizontal rather than upright.

**West of England** This, along with the Pilgrim, is thought to be the original or common goose of Britain during Victorian times. Goslings are sex-linked for colour, the female being grey or a mixture of grey and white, and the male plain white.

## HEAVY GEESE

**American Buff** Characterised by orange-buff feathers, with markings similar to the Toulouse (see below), the plumage is mainly fawn with a paler abdomen; the eyes are brown and it has orange feet and bill. It has been developed in the US through 40 years of selective breeding from the general farm goose. Very docile, it makes a good parent.

**Embden** One of the most popular table birds. The tallest of all the breeds, often standing more than 1m (3ft) high, with an extremely long body and neck. Plumage is plain white. Females can weigh 12.5kg (28lb), males up to 15.5kg (34lb).

**Toulouse** Like the Embden, this is another bird that was specially bred as a meat bird, particularly for use by producers of *pâté de fois gras*. Because of their large size, they can have trouble moving around and need to be kept on fairly flat ground. Gentle birds, they are good as pets. Normally grey, but occasionally in white and buff, the bill is orange-red and the feet are flesh-coloured.

# Turkeys

Rearing turkeys is not rocket science, but these birds do have a reputation for being difficult to keep. It's true that they need a lot more attention when they are small, and that they aren't as hardy as other types of poultry, but good husbandry and common sense will help minimise mortality. Engaging and inquisitive birds, it's hard not to find them appealing, and it can be difficult not to get attached to them.

## Choosing your turkeys

You might immediately plump for one of the old traditional breeds, but commercial strains of turkeys – the white-feathered birds that account for the majority of Christmas birds – should not be sniffed at. Although, for economic reasons, most of these hybrids will be raised indoors in intensive systems, they're just as suitable for free-ranging and the quality of the meat improves immeasurably.

The old-fashioned way of raising turkeys was to keep them locked in a building 24 hours a day, giving them as little opportunity as possible to move around and waste energy, but few smallholders with integrity would dream of providing such a restrictive and miserable environment. The old adage, 'You are what you eat' is true, but it must also be said that where, when, and how the birds eat is equally as important. So do not discount the white birds if you see them on offer – try them outdoors, allow them to graze, and see how much better the meat tastes compared to the super-cheap supermarket birds.

White hybrids are the most popular with commercial farmers.

Turkey breed names normally refer to their plumage – Norfolk black, bronze, white, buff, bourbon red, and blue or slate – though the Cröllwitzer, which is a striking white bird with black banding, is an exception. Generally, if you're looking for turkeys to rear for meat, you're only going to be offered black, bronze, or white, although the smaller and rarer bourbons are now growing in popularity due to high-end supermarkets promoting them as a niche product.

As mentioned above, commercial turkeys given a free-range lifestyle taste far better than those intensively reared. However, there's also a world of difference between the meat of white turkeys and that of the more traditional varieties. Demand for bronze and black turkeys has grown steadily over the past few years, thanks to top TV chefs praising their superior flavour.

Until the 1950s, most turkeys were bronze or black, with only the occasional white 'mutant'. However, in the name of economy, fast-growing commercial hybrids, which were cheaper to produce, began to emerge. They took less feed because they reached slaughter weight in half the time it took the traditional varieties. The customers liked them because not only were they cheaper to buy, they also looked neater when dressed, as no matter how meticulous the plucker, dark feathers leave dark quills in the skin.

Today, taste is once again triumphing over cheapness and presentation. Traditional breeds are more closely related to the original wild turkeys, and consequently are slower-growing and reach smaller weights. You can order light or heavy strains, but they only vary by a few kilos. The average bird will reach between 5.4kg (12lb) and 6.8kg (15lb) – ample for most families – within 20 to 24 weeks.

## Turkeys for Christmas

If you're unsure about brooding young birds, you'll be best off buying growers – these are young birds of about six weeks' old, which are fully-feathered and therefore need less care and attention. It's cheaper – and, in some ways, can be more satisfying – to raise them from day-old poults, but much more challenging and time-consuming.

You will have to order your birds well in advance (check the classified advertisements in specialist magazines for dealers who will deliver), because there aren't many breeders who will supply small numbers. Orders are usually taken in the spring, with the birds being delivered late summer. Make sure that the birds you order will reach the target weight by your projected slaughter date.

Large hatcheries will normally offer a choice of stags or hens, with hens being the more expensive. Stags will, of course, give you larger birds (unless you restrict their feeding), but more people opt for the smaller, family-sized turkeys these days.

## Caring for poults

If you choose to buy day-old poults, they will normally be delivered straight from the hatchery in a specially designed cardboard box featuring four compartments.

Day-old poults arriving by courier.

### HEAT AND WARMTH

The poults will need constant heat from the minute you take them out of the box, so overhead infra-red lamps are a must. Small numbers can be put into tailor-made brooder cages or boxes, but larger numbers will be more easily accommodated in a secure shed with a floor covered in wooden shavings. Whatever you choose, make sure the lamps are turned on an hour or so before the arrival of the birds.

Young birds in a brooder cage.

Poults under a heat lamp.

Tiny poults need a tremendous amount of heat in order to simulate the warmth provided by the underbelly of a mother turkey hen. The temperature needs to stay around 35°C for the first two weeks of their lives, gradually decreasing as they get older, but you have to watch their behaviour and adjust the height of the brooder lamps accordingly; too warm and you'll see the birds gasping; too cold and they'll huddle together for warmth, often smothering one another in the process.

With turkey poults, the biggest cause of death in the early weeks is not sickness, but smothering. As they clamber on top of one another for warmth, some will end up at the bottom of the pile, so be vigilant and adjust the heat accordingly.

Drowning is also a danger, so make sure you have purpose-made chick drinkers, such as the balloon-shaped kind which you unscrew, invert, fill with water, screw onto the base, and then stand the right way up. These let just enough water out into the 'moat' in the base, which is too shallow for poults to drown in.

Some people believe that turkey poults can die of fright. It is true that they can be easily scared by loud and sudden noises, and one tried and tested procedure is leaving a radio on in the brooding shed to help calm them. It also partly muffles the sound of outside noises and of the door being opened and closed.

## Health

The risk of early mortality deters many people from rearing turkeys, as it's not nice going down to the shed in the morning, only to have to pick up another tiny dead body. Generally, if your poults do not die in the first four weeks, they stand a good chance of survival. Experts say you should expect to lose at least 10% in the first month, either through suffocation from huddling or general, unexplained fading.

Once they are fully-feathered and out to grass, there should be little to worry about – apart from the deadly disease known as blackhead (see box). Birds lose interest in food, droppings turn yellow and runny, and there is often a darkening of the skin and wattles before they eventually die.

These fully-feathered birds are outdoors, but still need to be housed at night.

Turkeys can thrive in extremely cold temperatures.

### How to avoid blackhead disease

Blackhead – histomoniasis, to give it its proper name – is a disease which attacks the digestive tract of turkeys. Chickens and some wild birds can carry the disease without being affected by it, and it can lie dormant in the soil for years. The usual advice given is never to keep chickens and turkeys together. However, for people with restricted space that just isn't practical. The key rule is to make sure you worm your hens regularly, as Heterakis gallinae (the caecal roundworm) is to blame for the problem. As visiting garden birds can also carry the worm, it pays to keep your feed and water containers indoors if at all possible.

Once fully-grown, turkeys are pretty hardy creatures, and can withstand severe extremes of weather. It isn't uncommon to see them roosting in mid-winter with snow on their backs. They don't do well in wet weather, and you might have a battle on your hands trying to get them to shelter. They may stubbornly want to stay outdoors, but they're more prone to ailments in wet weather, so try and get them indoors if you possibly can.

### Feeding

Turkeys should not be treated like other poultry when it comes to feeding. They do not thrive well enough on rations designed for chickens when they are very young, though these feeds can be used in an emergency.

Talk to your local feed merchant well in advance of getting your poults, as not all outlets consider it worthwhile stocking turkey feed on the off-chance of a customer calling by. Depending on how many birds you plan to rear, it might pay to have a bulk order delivered direct from the manufacturers. Bear in mind that to qualify for a discount you'll normally have to order a minimum of a tonne – about 40 bags weighing 25kg (55lb). This takes up quite a bit of space, and you'll also have to keep it dry and safe from vermin.

Like all young birds, turkey poults need to be started off on high-protein crumbs – but they should be the kind specifically designed for turkeys, containing between 24% and 28% protein. They will contain an anti-coccidiostat – a medication which protects against coccidiosis, which is a disease caused by an internal parasite. Starter crumbs can be fed until about six to eight weeks, after which they will move onto a grower ration, which is in pellet form. The best way to make the switch is by gradually mixing crumbs and pellets together, so the birds get used to the new texture.

Later, the birds should be moved on to a finishing diet. This is a pellet feed of a much lower protein – commonly around 16% protein – and they can stay on this from around 12 to 14 weeks old until slaughter. Feeds from different manufacturers will vary in composition, so ask your feed merchant for advice or contact the local representative for your chosen brand.

Some textbooks suggest that turkey poults are notoriously difficult to encourage to start eating and drinking. While this isn't entirely true, they certainly don't like eating straight off the floor when young. They don't have the natural habit of scratching around like chickens, so any spilled food just stays there and is wasted, which is particularly annoying as turkey food usually costs a lot more per bag than layers' pellets. Get yourself some spill-resistant feeders, and also make sure that whatever containers you use (you can get purpose-made chick feeders) are big enough for all the poults to feed at the same time, so they are not jockeying for position.

One of the great pleasures of rearing turkeys is seeing their reaction to new foods. Give them as varied a selection as possible – anything spare from the vegetable garden and green house, or reduced at the supermarket. Depending on what's available, they can be feasting on a wide range from peppers and pumpkins to broccoli and broad beans. Turkeys can see colours, so it is good to give them a bright array of treats from time to time to help relieve the boredom.

## Accommodation

Living accommodation for turkeys is simple. A pole barn – a three-sided structure, open to the elements on one side – is all that most require. As mentioned earlier, turkeys do not seem to feel the cold, so don't be surprised if your best efforts are ignored. However, if the weather does turn really bad, you might have to force your birds indoors, so plan how you might do it.

Turkeys love to roost, so provide them with some alternatives, which will discourage them from attempting to perch on the perimeter fence. A few scaffolding poles or wooden posts fixed together make an excellent perch, but make sure their wings are clipped to ensure they don't launch themselves off the perch and over the fence. A livestock trailer with perches fitted inside can be useful, offering shelter and a place where food can be left.

If you don't plan to lock up your turkeys overnight, you'll need a secure paddock, which should be fenced with small gauge wire and, if possible, bordered by an electric fence to deter foxes from digging underneath.

Turkeys enjoy roosting from an early age.

# Other birds

Once you have got the bird-keeping bug, chances are you'll end up with all sorts of varieties. Visiting poultry auctions opens up a world of possibilities, from tiny quail and noisy guinea fowl to other gourmet favourites like pheasants and partridges. When you've mastered the basics of brooding young birds, there will be no stopping you.

The great thing is that nothing need be a rare and expensive delicacy any longer when you can rear it yourself. Get yourself some good books, take advice from breeders wherever possible, and apply the same high standard of husbandry that you give your existing birds.

One word of warning, however: if you're thinking about keeping ornamental birds, try to steer away from peacocks. They often appear in livestock auctions, but buyers often live to regret their purchases. They may look beautiful but, as anyone who has lived in close proximity to some will know, they can be incredibly irritating with their piercing calls, and they can devastate a well-stocked flower border or vegetable patch in no time at all.

They can also do serious damage to relations with your neighbours. Paignton Zoo was forced to destroy some of its wandering flock in June 2007 following complaints from nearby residents, and similar neighbourhood disputes have erupted in many places across the UK.

*Peacocks may be attractive, but their noise could make you unpopular.*

Guinea fowl make great burglar alarms because they react loudly to intruders.

Quail eggs are often highly sought after by restaurants.

# BEES

Beekeeping is rapidly catching up in popularity with rearing poultry as one of the first ventures for smallholders. Hives take up little space, so can be fitted into the smallest of gardens, and they can be extremely productive.

Whether you're hoping to harvest your own honey and beeswax as a hobby, encourage more bees to your holding to help pollinate crops, or simply help boost the dwindling numbers and pay your contribution to nature conservation, beekeeping can be a fascinating activity to get involved in. The falling number of honey bees (Apis mellifera) has become a cause for serious concern in recent years, not least because of colony collapses in the UK and overseas due to factors such as pests and parasites, fungal or viral infections, use of insecticides and loss of suitable habitat.

## Getting started

Before spending a fortune on equipment, get a taste of what beekeeping is all about and decide if it's really for you. The British Beekeepers' Association should be able to provide you with contacts for members in your area and there are numerous local groups across the UK that organise talks, hands-on demonstrations, and educational courses which will help you make up your mind. A lot of groups offer membership packages for non-beekeepers,

which allow newcomers to get involved without paying the full cost.

If you can, arrange to spend some time with an established beekeeper. It's surprising how many people like the idea of managing hives, only to find that the work and commitment involved are too much for them.

**Beekeeping – particularly understanding how a colony works, the life cycle, roles, and characteristics of each participant – can be quite a complex subject, and is beyond the scope of this simple introduction. Claire and Adrian Waring's *Bee Manual* offers a complete guide to everything you need to know about beekeeping and clearly illustrates in pictures many things which other beekeeping books struggle to explain in words.**

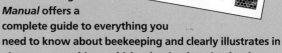

## Equipment and clothing

Knowledge and confidence are the key things, and once you have acquired these, you can move on to buying the essential kit you'll need. Specialist websites and catalogues offer a bewildering range of hives, protective clothing and other equipment, but there are a few basic items you must have if you want to care for a couple of colonies.

**Hives** You may be fortunate enough to buy or be given a hive or two by someone who is giving up beekeeping and, if the previous owner is knowlegeable and experienced and the hives are in good condition, this is often a good way to start. Associations will often advertise equipment for sale, which makes joining one an even more practical idea. There are numerous types of hive on the market.

In the UK, the most popular type is the Modified National, often just called the National. This is a wooden hive, but there are plastic and polystyrene models on the market too. Bees will live happily in any small cavity that's dry, secure and has a small entrance hole, but if you offer accommodation that is more attractive, they may be persuaded to move home. The reason there are so many different designs is that beekeepers are all different; some features will appeal to one person, but not to another. Look at as many different styles as you can, assess them for ease of use, and talk to beekeepers about why they chose their particular hives.

You can, of course, build your own hives, and plans are available in books and on the Internet, should your DIY skills and dedication be up to it. Recycled materials can be used, but select good quality materials of a decent weight.

**Protective clothing** If you look at some archive photographs of beekeepers handling colonies, you may see men in their shirtsleeves using no protective clothes whatsoever. Regardless of this, protective clothing is a must, so don't skimp on kitting yourself out.

Start with a good hat and veil. Again, just as there are many different styles of hive, there are different types of headgear to suit all tastes. See what other beekeepers are wearing, ask if you can try it on and decide what suits you best. Probably the simplest design is the traditional wide-brimmed hat with a veil attached that comes down over the shoulders and secures under the armpits. This is normally worn with a white boiler suit or a white tunic. A variation on the hat and veil is the Sherriff veil (named after its designer, Brian Sherriff). This is a spaceman-like creation comprising a series of horseshoe-shaped hoops covered with mesh which fold back when not in use.

Strong gloves should be worn, particularly when you're starting out – although it must be said that they make handling more tricky, and bees can sting through many types of materials.

*Invest in some decent protective clothing or you will regret it.*

National Bee Supplies

The National is one of the most popular hives in the UK.

**Smoker** Smoke is used to control bees because in the wild, smoke from a forest fire warns bees it's too dangerous to hang around. Their reaction is to feast on the honey stores, filling their bodies with food and enlarging the abdomen so it's less flexible. As a result, the bee cannot move its body so easily, and is less likely to sting. Designs vary, but all smokers will have a firebox in which to start burning paper, woodshavings, or whatever; a bellows which pumps out the smoke; and a nozzle from which the smoke emerges. When choosing a smoker, buy the biggest you can find – but make sure it is comfortable to use and not too big for your hand.

**Hive tool** Used for scraping off wax and other residue during cleaning and also for loosening and lifting hive components, the hive tool is a must-have gadget which comes in two basic types. The standard hive tool is a piece of metal that is flat at one end and curved at the other. The other type – the 'J' tool – also has one flat end, but gets its name from the J-shaped second end. Whichever style you choose, buy one with a thin end because it will be easier to use and will not cause as much damage to equipment as a thicker one.

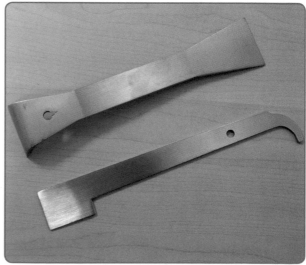

## Getting your bees

As with any living creatures, source your bees from a reputable person. You need to know that what you are buying or being given is free from disease. If in doubt, you should contact your Regional Bee Inspector, who works on behalf of the National Bee Unit and who oversees a team of Seasonal Bee Inspectors who are given their own patches to cover. There are some commercial suppliers in the UK, but most beginners start off by buying or acquiring some from a local beekeeper. Alternatively, you may be able to collect an unwanted swarm – though this isn't recommended for complete novices with little or no experience of handling bees. The correct procedure is explained in detail in the Haynes *Bee Manual*.

## Health

There are numerous health problems that can affect colonies, but two of the most destructive diseases, which are also notifiable by law to the National Bee Unit, are:

**American Foul Brood (AFB)** Not confined to the US – the name is linked to where the disease originated – AFB is caused by a bacterium. It's a fatal disease which attacks the bee's gut and is quickly spread via spores to other bees. There is no legal treatment for AFB and, once disease is confirmed, bees are destroyed.

**European Foul brood (EFB)** As with AFB, this is now an international disease, but not quite so damaging. The bacterium that causes it attacks the gut of developing larvae, rather like intestinal worms, so competing for food and eventually starving the larvae to death. Treatments are available in the case of a light infection, but more severe cases may lead to a colony being destroyed.

**Mites and other pests** There are various parasitic mites that have a detrimental effect on colonies. By far the most serious is Varroa destructor, which is present in most UK hives and survives by sucking bees' blood. Various chemical treatments are available, but all must be used with care. The Tropilaelaps mite is smaller than varroa, but its presence in a colony is more serious and must be notified to the National Bee Unit, as must any cases of Aethena tumida, the small hive beetle, whose larvae eats bee eggs and damage combs.

## Colony Collapse Disorder

This originated in the US and was responsible for the destruction of thousands of honey-bee colonies there. Colonies can be all but wiped out in a matter of weeks, with dead bees showing no apparent ailment.

### Siting the bee hive

**Consider the following points when siting a hive**
- **Easy access for the beekeeper.**
- **A position that will not annoy or concern neighbours or other members of the public.**
- **Shelter from strong winds and driving rain.**
- **Away from shade from overhanging trees.**
- **Firm ground with good drainage.**

Protect the apiary from livestock

# FOUR-LEGGED LIVESTOCK

Once you move on to keeping 'proper' animals, you start discovering the bureaucracy surrounding farming. It's all there for a good reason, of course, but you won't find anyone who enjoys filling in forms and keeping records.

The first bit of red tape, as explained in Chapter 3, is getting your holding registered, and acquiring flock and/or herd numbers for any sheep, goats, cattle, or pigs.

You'll have to start dealing with various government agencies, as well as your local trading standards department, which handles animal movement documentation and will issue you with forms which have to be completed every time stock are moved.

It's important to remember that you're shifting up a gear in livestock terms. Most of the time, rearing animals with feathers is a fairly easy business, requiring little in the way of veterinary expertise or physical effort. All kinds of livestock need routine maintenance, which requires new sets of skills and knowledge, so seek out some training before you decide to take on something you might not be able to handle. As

mentioned elsewhere in this book, it would be helpful if you could visit some neighbouring farmers. Then you can see for yourself the kind of regular duties you will be expected to perform – everyday things like handling and restraint, giving injections and oral medicines, caring for feet, and treating minor injuries.

You should, of course, find a good farm vet as early as possible. The vet will be happy to show you how to administer drugs and explain, for instance, the sites for different types of injections. Most of the time, you'll be expected to carry out tasks like this yourself, although the majority of vets will do the job for you if you insist.

You will probably feel happier calling out the vet for routine jobs the first couple of times, and you should always do so if you do not feel sufficiently confident. By the time subsequent treatments are needed, you may be ready to do the job yourself, which means getting hold of drugs from your vet. Most vets will not dispense certain drugs unless they have recently (at least in the past year) visited your stock.

## Notifiable diseases

Fortunately, major outbreaks of serious diseases are extremely rare, but some, like foot-and-mouth, BSE, bluetongue, bovine tuberculosis (bTB), and anthrax do appear from time to time.

Thankfully, the organisations with responsibility for dealing with such outbreaks learned some serious lessons following the disastrous foot-and-mouth outbreak of 2001. There was widespread criticism that restrictions put in place during the following outbreak in 2007 were far too stringent, but, in fairness to the authorities, it must be a difficult call to make when the safety of the bulk of the UK's livestock is potentially at risk.

Keeping farmers up-to-date with the latest information regarding animal movement restrictions is vitally important, and one innovative development in 2007 was the introduction of a system of sending updates as voice messages to mobile phones.

What can we, as farmers, do to protect our animals? Vaccination may be appropriate in some circumstances, but everything comes back to vigilance and good husbandry. That means keeping a close eye on your stock for changes in behaviour or appearance, and checking for telltale signs on a regular basis. It also means observing movement restrictions and employing high standards of biosecurity, both on your own farm and when visiting others.

### ISOLATION UNITS

Introducing new livestock to your farm is a high-risk activity if you already have some animals. Any new stock – particularly if bought from a market or auction – can carry infections and diseases. New arrivals should, therefore, be isolated until you are satisfied they are healthy and pose no risk. It's good practice to do this as a matter of course, rather than risk the health of the entire herd. For breeders who hire out or hire in stud animals, consider it essential to have a quarantine area.

### Why isolate?

- It allows the passage of the incubation period – the time it takes for symptoms of an illness to develop.
- It makes it easier to monitor, closely inspect, or treat the animals.
- It allows more freedom for moving stock on and off the farm.
- It just makes good sense – why take risks?

### GETTING AN APPROVED UNIT

It doesn't cost anything to have an existing building or outdoor area approved as an isolation unit. All you have to do is contact your local Animal Health office and an inspection will normally be carried out by your own or another local vet, who will provide a written report stating that the following criteria can be satisfied:

- The unit must only ever be used for isolation.
- It should ideally be a building separate from any other housing livestock.
- The floors and walls must be in good condition so they can be washed and disinfected.
- Disinfectant footbaths must be provided at the entrance.
- Staff must use dedicated protective clothing, and protective clothing should be provided for visitors.
- No other animals should come into contact with manure or effluent from the building.

### OUTDOOR ISOLATION UNITS ARE POSSIBLE, BUT:

- Paddocks must only ever be used for isolation.
- They must be physically separate from any land or buildings used for other livestock.
- There must be a minimum distance of 3m (10ft) between the perimeter of the isolation paddocks and any other livestock.

Isolation units give you more flexibility when moving livestock.

**ISOLATION UNIT**

The pigs in this barn have recently arrived and are being isolated for biosecurity reasons – to ensure they are healthy before joining the rest of the herd.

Please disinfect your boots before entering the building and when you leave, and remember to wash your hands.

# Sheep

**Lambs for slaughter** Sheep less than 12 months old that are being reared for meat and will be slaughtered before they reach a year, need only be identified with a single slaughter tag showing the flock number. This can be an EID, if you wish, but it's not compulsory. However, some abattoirs and marts insist on an EID for their own operational purposes, so check locally before you tag.

**Older sheep** At the time of writing (2012), there is no need to electronically identify older animals which were already tagged before December 31, 2009. They can currently be kept with two matching conventional tags (or a tag in one ear and a breed society tattoo in the other). However, from 31 December 2014, these too will have to be fitted with electronic tags with individual identification numbers.

**When to tag** Tagging of new sheep must take place before sheep reach nine months of age (before six months if housed overnight), or before they leave the holding of birth – whichever comes sooner.

Breed societies will have their own additional rules on identification in respect of pedigree breeding stock, so check with them regarding tattooing or notching.

## Movement

Keepers must inspect sheep for signs of disease before movement. Any signs of notifiable diseases (e.g. foot and mouth) must be reported to the local Animal Health and Veterinary Laboratories Agency (AHVLA).

All sheep, goat and deer movements must be accompanied by a completed animal movement licence (AML1). There are four duplicate pages to each document – one white, one pink, one blue and one yellow. Details must be completed by both the departure premises (i.e. where the animals were kept) and the destination premises.

Newcomers to smallholding often assume that sheep are easy to keep. It is amazing how many people think it's merely a question of putting a few animals in the field to keep the grass down and letting them get on with it. Sheep are deceptive creatures: people see them roaming the hills in all weathers and believe they look after themselves. Guess what? They don't!

Sheep can be high-maintenance creatures. For a start, their feet will always need regular trimming, they'll need worming, and there are a whole host of other ailments, diseases and assorted health problems which will have to be taken care of. You'll need to learn how to administer drugs, both orally and by injection.

## Identification and movement

Sheep need to be tagged for identification purposes. All sheep born since January 2010 which are kept beyond 12 months of age – whether breeding stock or pets – have to be identified using two tags. One ear must carry a yellow electronic identification tag (EID), while the other ear can have a standard, non-electronic, plastic slaughter tag. Both must carry the same individual ID number, as well as the flock number.

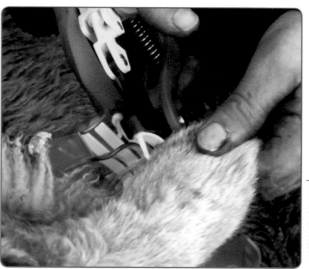

One ear must carry a yellow EID tag.

www.roxan.co.uk

The person receiving the animals must send the white copy to the trading standards department of his or her local authority within three days of the movement taking place. The pink copy is kept by the person receiving the animals, the blue copy is for the haulier, and the yellow copy is kept by the departure premises. Any movement of sheep onto your land triggers a 'standstill' – which means nothing can leave your holding until the relevant standstill time is up, apart from animals going direct to slaughter. In practice, this means that sheep, goats, cattle and deer are restricted for six days and pigs are restricted for 20 days.

## Keeping a flock book

All sheep and goat keepers are obliged to keep a flock/herd register, which contains details of animals kept on the holding, movements on and off, births and deaths. These details can be kept in a variety of forms. Agricultural suppliers sell flock and herd books, although trading standards departments will normally supply sheets for you to fill in and store in a file. Alternatively, details can be stored on computer.

In addition to keeping your own records, you will also be sent an annual sheep and goat inventory to complete, in which you will be required to list details of how many animals you currently have.

## Keeping sheep – the simple way

If you've decided that you really do want sheep, the next decision is at what you want them for and at what age to buy them. Some people just like the idea of sheep on their land. Estate agents reckon the sight of an attractive flock of sheep grazing happily could add as much as £10,000 to the price of a house. Hard to imagine? It's all about buying the dream.

If all you want are lawnmowers that look nice on pastureland in front of the house, why not think about inviting someone else's sheep in for occasional grazing? It is the most hassle-free way of keeping sheep, with few responsibilities other than making sure your boundary fences are secure and keeping an eye on the flock to ensure there are not any welfare problems you should tell the owner about.

For generations, hill farmers have sent sheep away 'on tack' to lower-lying holdings to avoid the worst of the winter weather, collecting them once the spring grass has started to grow back at home. You could gain a useful source of income by offering grazing, or you could choose to be paid in meat.

If you really want a flock of your own, there are some other alternatives that will allow you to savour the excitement of being a sheep farmer while, at the same time, avoiding all that messy birthing business and other nasty jobs like the tricky business of castration. One option is buying ewe lambs in the autumn that can then be sold on as breeding ewes the next year.

A movement document for sheep and goats.

A flock book recording arrivals and departures.

The annual sheep and goat inventory.

## Filling the freezer

If your aim is to raise meat for the table, or to sell on to others, it is worth thinking about simply buying in ready-weaned lambs to fatten for slaughter. This can be done quickly or slowly, depending on your circumstances, needs and preferences. Some farmers buy in lambs towards the end of July or beginning of August and aim to finish them (get them to the required weight) in less than three months. Others prefer to let their lambs grow at a slower rate, sending them for slaughter in the spring at heavier weights.

There are some benefits to buying in lambs when there are lots of them flooding the market in about October or November and rearing them for the early spring market – before the 'new season' lamb is ready. The drawback of this is that your grass will not be at its best through the winter months, so you will have to feed some kind of supplement to make sure they get the nutrition they need.

When it comes to determining whether a lamb is ready for slaughter, you need to 'condition score' the animal, which involves placing your hand over the backbone in the area just behind the rib cage. Ask your vet or a friendly farmer to show you how it is done.

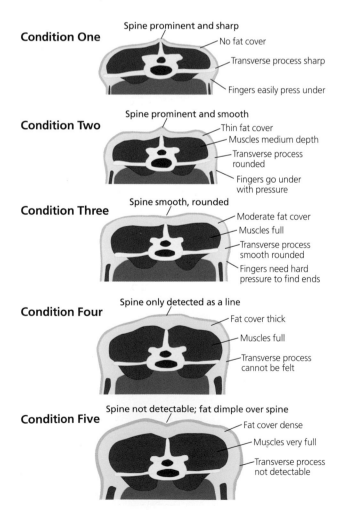

**Condition One**
Spine prominent and sharp
– No fat cover
– Transverse process sharp
– Fingers easily press under

**Condition Two**
Spine prominent and smooth
– Thin fat cover
– Muscles medium depth
– Transverse process rounded
– Fingers go under with pressure

**Condition Three**
Spine smooth, rounded
– Moderate fat cover
– Muscles full
– Transverse process smooth rounded
– Fingers need hard pressure to find ends

**Condition Four**
Spine only detected as a line
– Fat cover thick
– Muscles full
– Transverse process cannot be felt

**Condition Five**
Spine not detectable; fat dimple over spine
– Fat cover dense
– Muscles very full
– Transverse process not detectable

There is a scale of one to five: one is extremely thin and five is very fat. Three – right in the middle of the scale – is just right. Ewes are often scored several times during the year – the most important time being five to six weeks before lambing. This is a crucial time for the growth of the unborn lamb and feeding should be adjusted according to the ewe's condition.

## Buying your first sheep

Always buy from a reputable breeder. Ask your farming neighbours for recommendations or contact the relevant breed society if you have a particular breed in mind. As with all animals, it's best to choose a breed that's well suited to the conditions on offer, so again, ask for advice.

**Follow the basic rules for buying an animal in good health, outlined earlier in this chapter. Watch for:**

- a sickly appearance and poor posture
- discharge from eyes or nose
- scouring (diarrhoea)
- poor coat/skin and scratching
- coughing or sneezing
- lameness or other signs of pain or discomfort.

When choosing both sheep and goats, feet and teeth require particular scrutiny. If you buy a sheep with badly overgrown or misshapen feet, you may not be able to rectify the damage by trimming. Take someone with you who knows what to look out for. Get them to look over the udders at the same time, checking for lumps or problems with the teats.

The approximate age of a sheep can be determined by looking at its teeth. Lambs are born with eight milk teeth, then between 12 and 15 months old, the first two permanent incisors erupt at the front of the mouth. The next two appear on either side of the first pair about a year later. The next two – again, either side of the existing ones – arrive when the sheep are about two years and three months old, and two more will be seen about six months later.

As the sheep grows older, its teeth will gradually wear and loosen, leaving what farmers call a 'broken-mouthed ewe' – or simply a 'broker'. These ewes can carry on producing lambs for many years, but the lack of teeth may mean they cannot eat as well as they used to and they are likely to need extra care and attention to ensure they and their unborn lambs receive sufficient nutrition.

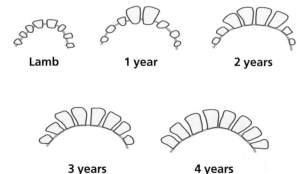

Lamb        1 year        2 years

3 years        4 years

## Choosing breeds

When you are starting out, it is best to choose the kind of sheep your experienced farming neighbours already have. Chances are, they have been keeping them for generations because they suit the climate and terrain. More often than not, they will be cross-bred, and their parents will have been chosen for specific reasons. A big Texel or Suffolk ram may, for instance, be mated with a smaller breed to help produce a meatier carcass. Alternatively, a breed with a smaller head and shoulders may be used if the aim is to produce lambs that are easier to deliver.

Having said all this, you may have long-term plans to build up a pedigree flock. As with most things, personal preferences differ hugely, and there are so many breeds to choose from, you will be spoiled for choice. Do your research, consider which breeds will do best in your particular area, and get in touch with breed societies to find suppliers in your area.

Bear in mind that, if you opt for a rare breed or one which isn't already reared locally, you could hit problems when you want to start breeding, because getting access to fresh bloodlines might be a problem. If you have only a small flock, you will constantly be on the lookout for unrelated rams, and you could find yourself trekking hundreds of miles to find a suitable match.

This section includes a few breeds to start thinking about. Refer to the books and websites suggested at the end of this section, visit agricultural shows and sales, and do plenty of research before you make your choice.

**Badger Face (right)** Good to start with as they are small, hardy and fairly easy to handle. There are two types of badger face: torddu and torwen. In Welsh, torddu means black belly. The fleece can be white, grey or light brown, always with distinctive black markings. There are black stripes above the eyes and a wide black stripe that starts under the chin and continues under the belly and right to the end of the tail. The legs are black with a tan stripe. The torwen ('white belly') is almost a negative of the torddu, with reverse colouring.

**Balwen (right)** Another manageable and hardy breed, this is one of the original Welsh sheep. The breed came from the Tywi valley in Carmarthenshire and was almost wiped out in the 1940s by a disastrous winter which left just one ram. It's still classed as a rare breed. Predominantly black, dark brown, or dark grey, it has a white stripe running from the top of the head to the top of the nose, hence the name balwen (white blaze). The feet are white and there is white on the tail. It's renowned for having good feet and being an easy lamber.

**Beltex** A strong, double-muscled sheep from Belgium used in cross-breeding to improve carcass quality. Created by selective breeding, it is popular with commercial producers not only for its ability to produce offspring with meaty, fine-boned bodies, but also ewes that give birth with ease.

Oogie McGuire

**Black Welsh Mountain (Above)** A handsome sheep with a fleece which is thick and easy to handle and doesn't need to be dyed. The breed carries a dominant black gene, so even when cross-bred the offspring is black. They are hardy and undemanding and do not normally need supplementary feeding, being content to eat short, rough grasses.

**Bluefaced Leicester (Left)** The majority of cross-bred ewes (known as 'mules') in the UK are thought to have been sired by Bluefaced Leicester rams. They can be used to serve any breed of ewe to help improve conformation, birth rates and milk yields, and are a popular choice to cross with hill breeds.

**British Texel** Famous for its exceptional carcass qualities and hardiness, the Texel is one of the most popular terminal sire breeds in Europe. Texel ewes can raise twins without much additional feeding and they do well in areas of poor vegetation, such as on upland pastures.

**Hebridean (Left)** One of the primitive breeds of Scotland and the Western Isles, the Hebridean is relatively small and fine boned, with black or dark brown wool, a short, triangular tail and often two pairs of long horns. Hardy and able to thrive on rough grazing, they're used extensively in conservation grazing, to maintain natural grassland or heathland, or to clear scrub.

**Herdwick** Native to the central and western Lake District, these hardy sheep live on hills up to 900m (3,000ft) high in an area with the UK's heaviest rainfall. Excellent foragers, they do not need supplementary feeding, even when grazing is poor. Born black, the lambs lighten to dark brown after the first year, eventually turning to grey. Rams have horns, but the ewes are polled.

**Hill Radnor** The Hill Radnor is a heavy, hardy breed found mainly in Powys, mid-Wales. It has a tan-coloured face and legs, which are free from wool, and small, alert ears. The dense fleece is popular with hand-spinners and weavers. The ewes are good mothers and the breed is good for crossing.

**Jacob** This breed takes its name from the Old Testament tale of how Jacob became a selective breeder of pied sheep. A very popular breed with first-time sheep-keepers because of its relatively small size and attractive brown and white fleece, which produces high-quality wool, sought-after for spinning and weaving. The tanned skins also sell well as rugs.

**Lleyn (Right)** A hardy, medium-sized breed that gets its name from the peninsular on Anglesey, where it originated. Easy and prolific lambers, the ewes are good mothers. The wool is white and dense and of good quality and the body is wide-breasted with a long back.

**Shropshire (Right)** This medium-sized breed is the result of selective breeding from the indigenous sheep of the Staffordshire and Shropshire border areas. Popular with tree-growers because they graze without damaging bark, they are often used in orchards and Christmas tree plantations.

**Soay** The most primitive looking of all sheep found in the UK, the Soay is a small breed which weighs around 25kg (55lb) when fully grown. The fleece comes in shades of brown with light markings under the belly, on the rump, over the eyes and under the jaw. Rams are usually horned, but ewes can be born with or without. Like the Hebridean, it is used in conservation grazing. The breed is classified as 'at risk' by the Rare Breeds Survival Trust.

**Suffolk** Another popular terminal sire breed because, as scientific studies have shown, its growth rate is second to none. A fairly large breed with a long black face, the Suffolk has a high milk yield, strong hooves, and ewes have wide pelvises, making lambing easier.

**Welsh Mountain (Right)** Probably a bit too much of a challenge for the complete beginner, the Welsh Mountain is a nervous, flighty sheep, but, nevertheless, a reliable breed, well-conditioned to withstand all kinds of harsh weather. It has a white or tan face and a strong, dense fleece. There are North and South Wales varieties. The South Wales Mountain is bigger and usually has tan markings on the face and legs, as well as a brown collar.

A ewe after shearing.

## Shearing and fly strike

Shearing has to be done, partly to keep your sheep comfortable in warmer temperatures, but just as importantly, in order to avoid the nightmare of fly strike, also known as blowfly strike. It's mainly caused by greenbottles and bluebottles, which are most active in mild weather when they're searching for places to lay their eggs. Fly strike can lead to death within days if untreated.

Unsheared adult sheep are prime targets, but lambs, goats and camelids can also be targeted. Pour-on insecticides, such as Vetrazin, Clik or Crovect, should be applied as soon as the mild weather begins and the animals should be sheared as soon as is practical to do so.

Any open wounds, signs of foot rot (see Health), or dirty fleeces should be taken care of to prevent the flies being attracted. The aroma of foot rot is particularly alluring. Sheep

with foot rot often get fly strike halfway down their sides, because when they lie down, their feet rub against this part of the fleece. Any animal that is lying down as a result of injury or illness is also extremely vulnerable.

Eggs can hatch in a matter of hours in the right conditions. Newly hatched maggots waste no time in nibbling their way at the sheep's flesh. Telltale signs to watch for include the sheep twisting its head round to try and reach the irritated area, stamping its hind feet, or repeatedly wagging its tail.

The affected sheep has to be caught, clipped, maggots removed, and the area cleaned and treated. A pour-on insecticide, as mentioned earlier, should be applied to deter a secondary strike. Some products have the ability to also kill maggots when applied to the affected area. Various other preparations are available which will kill the maggots as well as helping to heal the wound. Maggot oil is a particularly soothing preparation that seems to make affected sheep feel a lot more comfortable. If the animals are destined for the food chain, be sure to check the withdrawal times on any products you use, as there will be a specified period that must elapse before they can be slaughtered for meat.

## Learning to shear

The British Wool Marketing Board runs courses from time to time (which may be eligible for grant aid), and agricultural colleges may also provide training. Be warned, it is physical work; you not only have to catch your sheep, but also turn it on its back and hold it securely between your legs while you bend down to shear it on each side. Don't be surprised if your first attempt leaves you aching all over and walking like John Wayne for a while, because you will be using muscles you have probably never used before – or, at least, not for a long time. In addition, you will end up covered in grease from the lanolin produced by the sheep's sebaceous glands in order to waterproof the fleece – and you will not smell very good, either.

Shearing is not just about physical strength, it is also about confidence. Watch the professional shearing teams competing at agricultural shows and you will see them working like lightening with potentially lethal electrical cutting machinery. When you are starting off, it is difficult not to be over-cautious and hesitant, as no one wants to nick the skin of some poor, unsuspecting sheep and see blood.

Until you feel sufficiently happy about doing the job yourself, it may be best to hire someone in, or ask a neighbouring farmer to do yours when he or she is shearing. Whatever you decide to do, don't leave it too late, or you will regret it.

Ask someone to teach you about crutching and dagging sheep – the simple technique of hand-clipping any dirty wool around the tail and anus and between the legs. If you do have to wait your turn to get your sheep done by a professional shearer, you will at least be able to minimise the risk of fly strike by removing some of the most obvious targets.

## Sheep wool

If you live in the UK and have four or more adult sheep, the Wool Marketing Scheme requires you to register with the British Wool Marketing Board (BWMB) to market your fleece wool. Registration forms are available on application to the Producer Registration and Payments Department of the BWMB. You will be sent an explanation of the central marketing system and details of the wool depot authorised to handle your wool. Don't get excited, though – fleeces are worth pennies rather than pounds, and payment depends on quality.

Some rare breeds are exempt from the scheme, allowing farmers to sell in other ways, such as direct to spinners.

## Feeding

Sheep, like goats and cattle, are ruminants – cud-chewing animals with complex digestive systems. This means they can process foods that other animals can't, such as tough plant material like grasses and tree branches. Huge quantities can be swallowed with a minimum of chewing. Later when the animal is resting, it is regurgitated, re-chewed and broken up into smaller pieces for digestion. All ruminants have four-chambered stomachs; the rumen (hence the name ruminant) is the largest, and contains the micro-organisms that secrete enzymes to break down the cellulose in the plant cell walls so that nutrients can be absorbed.

Most of the time, sheep can derive the nutrition they need from the pasture, but during the winter, when grazing is poor, they may also need hay, silage, root crops, or other bagged feeds. At certain times of the year, such as coming up to tupping (mating) and during pregnancy and lactation, supplementary feed should be given. Vitamin and mineral licks sold in large tubs or in blocks are designed to combat nutritional deficiencies and can be left out in the fields to be used as needed.

## Health
### FOOT CARE

Probably the biggest problem sheep farmers have is lameness in the flock. Sheep feet are not the best of designs. Each foot is split into two pads or cleats, and the gap in between is a lovely, warm place where bacteria can thrive and cause foot rot, a painful ailment which is often only spotted when a sheep is seen limping. Although curable, it is better not to have to treat it in the first place. Scald is another uncomfortable condition, caused by long grass irritating the skin between the cleats.

You cannot be lazy with foot care. Feet have to be inspected at regular intervals and trimmed as level as possible, otherwise the sheep can become extremely uncomfortable and this will eventually affect overall condition.

The hooves grow at different rates according to environmental conditions, weather, terrain and nutrition. With a small flock, it should be possible to inspect the feet every month or so to keep a check on growth. Once a hoof has started to grow into an awkward shape, it can be difficult or sometimes impossible to correct.

### TEETH

The loss of teeth due to old age does not necessarily mean a sheep has come to the end of its usefulness. A ewe with missing teeth may need additional feed and nutritional supplements in order to keep on producing healthy lambs, but many smallholders become attached to their older ewes and are prepared to let them live out their days. As long as they do not have to compete for food with others, and have no debilitating health problems, retired sheep can live quite happily to a ripe old age. A surprising number of herds have a favourite ewe that is 15 to 20 years old.

### MASTITIS

This condition is caused by a bacterial infection and affects a wide range of species. It causes painful swelling lumps in the udder which must be treated with antibiotics and anti-inflammatory drugs. If left untreated, severe cases of mastitis can kill. Although you may not be planning to breed sheep just yet, you may end up buying some ewes with lambs at foot (still suckling), or some newly weaned ewes, either of which can be affected.

### INTERNAL PARASITES

Intestinal worms are a common problem for most sheep farmers. All sheep will carry some roundworms. Eggs get passed out of the body in the faeces, the larvae hatch and are eaten by other sheep, and they cause a loss of condition. Thin and young ewes may need to be drenched (given an oral dose of a wormer) as a precaution at tupping time, but ewes are generally treated after lambing.

Grazing ewes on clean pasture is the best way of controlling worms, but not always possible. One way of minimising the risk of infection is to keep just a few sheep per acre. Two to three is generally recommended, but this will vary depending on the type of land and the time of year. Another good practice is to allow grazing on fields in alternate years. A mixed grazing regime – using cattle as well as sheep – can also help reduce the number of larvae which get back into the sheep's body when grazing.

The modern approach to worming is only to do so when necessary, as sheep can build up a resistance to drugs used too regularly. However, when introducing new sheep to a flock, most farmers will worm as a precaution.

**Tapeworms** live in the small intestine of the sheep and, although they look horrible when excreted, normally cause little harm to the animal, as sheep are only intermediate hosts while the worms are growing.

**Liver fluke** may be a problem in wet and boggy areas. The fluke is a parasite which uses a mud snail as a host to help it reproduce. The immature fluke is found on grass and, when eaten by the sheep, makes its way to the liver, causing severe anaemia, loss of condition, and death. Drugs that kill the adult fluke are available, but some are less effective on immature ones, so discuss treatment with your vet.

### EXTERNAL PARASITES

**Sheep scab** is the result of a mite that causes widespread problems. The mites burrow under the skin, causing severe irritation and leaving a scab. The infection can spread rapidly and, even when shearing has taken place, the mites can survive by hiding in folds of skin. Routine dipping of sheep is not carried out as regularly nowadays, as farmers have found their flocks build up a resistance if done too frequently. Infected sheep can be treated by injection.

## Disbudding, castration and tail docking

These are controversial subjects and carrying out such procedures is largely a matter of choice, but there are restrictions as to who can do what and when.

If you choose a horned breed of sheep and disbudding is required, it must be carried out by a veterinary surgeon, and it must be done within the first 10 days of birth, ideally within the first two to three days.

If you are just concentrating on buying in and rearing weaned lambs for the freezer at the moment, you will not need to worry about castrating or tail docking newborns, but you may end up buying some that haven't been done and that will need veterinary assistance.

Castration is normally carried out for management reasons, so that ram lambs can be grown in groups without fighting, and also alongside ewe lambs without the risk of inbreeding. Tail docking is done to help keep the back end of the sheep as free as possible from faeces, and therefore lessen the risk of fly strike. A long tail gets in the way and quickly becomes soiled.

The law says that once the ewe and lamb have bonded, a rubber elastrator ring can be applied to the scrotum or tail by a competent, trained person, but it must be done in the first week of life. After that time, it must be carried out with anaesthetic. Furthermore, after three months of age, castration can only be carried out by a vet, as a surgical procedure, again using a suitable anaesthetic.

### Orphaned lambs – be warned!

Photographs of tiny orphan lambs being bottle-reared can tear at the heartstrings and bring out the nurturing instinct in us all. You will often find that farmers are only too glad to give away orphaned lambs – simply because bottle-feeding them round the clock and keeping them warm under an infra-red lamp is too much like hard work when you have maybe hundreds or thousands of ewes lambing and a busy farm business to run. If they aren't keen to take milk from a bottle, they may even need 'tubing' – feeding by inserting a tube down the throat and directly into the stomach. Hand-rearing any animal is a demanding job, but also very satisfying when you know that, but for your intervention, it would certainly have died.

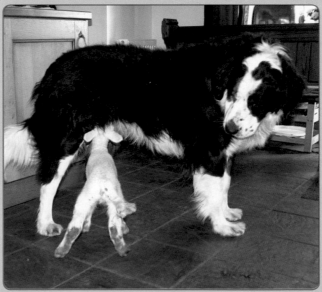

This orphan lamb grew up with the family pets for company

# Goats

There is an old Arab proverb that says, 'Let he who is without problems get a goat.' This may be a slight exaggeration, but it is important not to underestimate how much time and attention goats demand, particularly in terms of keeping them in one place so that they do not destroy everything in sight.

Goats are incredibly intelligent, friendly and entertaining. They can be immensely satisfying to keep, and they produce meat, milk and fibre for spinning. However, rather like a weed is a flower in the wrong place, goats can be a nightmare when they are anywhere you do not want them to be. Good, strong fencing is essential.

As discussed in the previous section about sheep, you'll have to register your holding (see Chapter 3) and get a flock/herd number.

## Identification and movement of goats

Tagging rules are almost identical to those for sheep, with the exception that, where double tagging is required, there is no need for one of the tags to be an electronic identification tag (EID). However, if owners wish to use an EID, they can.

The process of moving goats is the same as that for sheep, and the same paperwork (AML1 form) is used. You will also need to keep a flock book and complete an annual Sheep and Goat Inventory.

## Your first goats

One important thing to bear in mind is that you shouldn't just keep one goat. You may only want one – or only have space for one – but goats are herd animals and need the company of their own kind. Most people start off with two females, a mother and kid, two sisters, or often two that are completely unrelated.

As with most animals, there is a definite pecking order and one will inevitably be 'top goat'. You will not be able to change this, so do not try, though you might think about feeding them separately to make sure the bossiest one does not eat everything. If, later on, you decide to add another goat or two to the herd, be prepared for some initial problems with bullying. Things will eventually settle down and, as with most other animals, new goats will find their place in the hierarchy.

## Fencing

It used to be commonplace to tether goats to one spot, but it's a cruel and frustrating practice that can put them at risk of serious injury. Secure stock fencing is a must, and you need to make sure it's high enough to deter your goats from attempting to jump or clamber over. Normal height sheep fencing won't do – they'll be up and over before you know it – so make it at least 1.2m (4ft) high. Some people suggest putting a strand of barbed wire along the top of normal stock fencing, so the goats are

Goats will work hard to get the food they want.

## Sourcing goats

Agricultural shows are excellent places for getting to know about goats and meeting breeders face-to-face. Goat breeders are always happy to chat about their animals and to give advice to newcomers, so don't be afraid to ask. The British Goat Society (see Further Information, page 172) has contact details for all the breed societies.

When you come to viewing potential purchases, perform the same general health checks you would for any animal, as outlined earlier in this chapter, but if you've tracked down a reputable breeder, you should be in safe hands.

Before you take your goats away, ask the breeder to run through basic husbandry tasks, like foot trimming, giving veterinary treatments and milking. You should also have your goats' accommodation and feeding equipment ready before they arrive. Goats can be impatient, so don't keep them waiting.

## Accommodation

Goats hate the rain. Even a few spots send them scurrying for cover, so you'll need to arrange suitable shelter for when they are out during the day. A field shelter like those provided for horses will do, or you could use a calf hutch or something similar.

**Housing** The first rule is to find a place that is dry and free from draughts; goats cope well in cold weather, but they dislike being wet or in draughty conditions. Ideally, the housing should lead out onto a yard or a field so that the goats can be easily let out for exercise – otherwise you will have to attach dog or horse leads to their collars and lead them to and from their foraging area twice a day.

**Safety** The shed or building you intend to use, and its fittings, should be free from sharp edges. Similarly, take care when positioning hay to avoid injury, particularly to the eyes. Hay nets should not be used for goats with horns or for young kids, as they could get tangled. Check that the interior of the building isn't covered with lead paint, or any other paint or wood preservative that could be toxic to your goats.

**Security** If the animals are going to be locked in at night, the accommodation will need to be goat-proof. Don't think that a wooden shed will do, because they will quickly gnaw their way through it and smash unguarded windows with their feet. The ideal solution is a block-built stable. Be warned that goats are extremely clever and they quickly learn how to open latches and even bolts, so make sure your doors are securely locked on the outside.

**Food and water** The space devoted to food and water also needs careful consideration. Goats should have sufficient room to feed without having to push one another out of the way (although this will probably happen when the lead goat finishes her food). Water troughs or buckets should be positioned so that they can't be contaminated by droppings. Some agricultural merchants sell purpose-built simple bucket holders that can be fixed onto a wall or door, safely out of the line of fire.

discouraged from resting their feet on the top, but accidents can happen. If a goat is intent on getting out, it may throw caution to the wind, attempt a jump and seriously injure its udder in the process.

Electric fencing can be used to strip-graze by allowing grazing on one section at a time, moving the animals on as they exhaust the vegetation. If you don't have mains power where it's required and are using a battery-operated energiser instead, check the battery regularly, as animals can tell when the power fails.

When using a series of strands of electrified tape, it can take a while to work out how low the bottom strand needs to be to stop the goats limboing underneath, and how high the top one needs to be to stop them jumping over. Another drawback is that if the bottom strand is touching wet grass, the fence will short-circuit and be useless.

Any young or valuable trees will need to be protected. Make a triangular guard around each tree with wooden stakes and strong wire fencing. Also, make sure the guard is high enough to prevent the goats from reaching the lowest branches, because they not only eat them, they also lean on them with their front legs to pull them down to a more convenient position, often snapping whole boughs in the process.

feed, and at least half of their daily diet should be made up of forage alone. If they can't be left to fend for themselves, they'll need hay and silage (preferably maize silage), supplemented with a goat mix containing ingredients like maize, oats, barley, wheat, beans and peas. Coarse mixes are good, but some goats can be fussy, picking out only the bits they like, and so they may miss out on certain nutrients. Pelleted feeds may look dull and boring, but they are a one-stop shop and offer a balanced diet.

If you're letting your goats browse naturally, be aware that some plants and trees can be poisonous – the best-known include rhododendron, yew, laurel and bracken. Most of the time, goats seem instinctively to know what to eat and what to avoid – more so than other livestock – but it pays to be cautious about where you put them. Many experienced goat-keepers say it is best to regard all cultivated (non-native) garden plants as potentially toxic, so keep your goats out of your flowerbeds.

## Health

Goats share a wide variety of health problems with sheep (see Sheep, page 100–110). They need regular worming and their feet need regular trimming to prevent lameness. They can pick up parasites, such as ticks, fleas and lice, and, like sheep, they can suffer from mastitis. They can also be hit by fly strike, though the short fibre around the tail area is less likely to be contaminated by faeces, making them less obvious targets.

Feeding must be carried out with care. Make sure that you don't over-feed certain foods, like concentrated pellets, which can lead to digestive problems such as bloating, acidosis, and laminitis.

Over-feeding can, of course, cause obesity. As well as being very bad for the general health of the animal, this can also cause problems when trying to get a female into kid.

## Disbudding and castration

As with sheep, if you choose a horned breed and disbudding is required, it must be carried out by a veterinary surgeon within the first ten days of birth – ideally within the first two to three days. The Royal College of Veterinary Surgeons considers the act of disbudding to be a mutilation, but it's accepted that, for welfare and management reasons, it's often necessary in larger goat herds.

Castration is a matter of choice. If male kids are being raised for meat and will be sent for slaughter before they reach maturity, there should be no reason to castrate. Where they are to be kept on as pets or companion animals for other livestock, and not used for breeding, they should be castrated. As with lambs (see Sheep, page 100–110), this can be carried out by a competent person without anaesthetic, as long as the kids are less than seven days old. The same rubber elastrator rings used for ram lambs can be used for goats. Castration after the kid is a week old can only be performed with anaesthetic and, after three months, this must be carried out by a vet, again using anaesthesia.

**Bedding** Dry bedding, such as straw or bark chippings, is essential and must be changed regularly; solid floors should be well-drained, because goats can expel huge amounts or urine. Damp floors can harbour bacteria that can contribute to foot rot, leading to lameness.

**Milking area** If you are planning to milk your goats, you will need a separate area for milking, which must be well-ventilated and easy to clean. Food safety laws are strict, and if you intend selling your milk, even on a small scale, your premises will have to be inspected and registered before you can begin trading. Contact the environmental health department and trading standards departments of your local council for information.

## Feeding

A balanced diet and constant supply of fresh water are essential. Like sheep, goats are ruminants, so they take in lots of tough old stuff very quickly and deal with it later (see the previous section on sheep).

Goats are browsers by nature, and love nothing more than foraging for their own food. The way they have evolved over the years means they need a huge amount of bulky

### Do I need a billy goat?

Refer back to the section on hens and cockerels, ducks and drakes, and the same advice applies: unless you're seriously into breeding, don't bother. If you need a billy goat for mating, find an experienced local breeder and take your nannies to be served. Entire (uncastrated) male goats can be difficult to handle for beginners and they can be aggressive.

## Choosing breeds

**Anglo Nubian (Right)** Milk from this breed is high in both butterfat and protein, so it is a popular choice with cheese and yoghurt makers. A good dual-purpose (milk and meat) breed, it has a very distinctive, convex Roman nose and long, droopy ears. The coat is short and silky and comes in a wide range of colours.

**Angora** Angoras have long, coarse, curly coats, which produce the highly prized mohair. With age, the coat develops ringlets and needs a fair amount of attention to keep it in good condition. Angoras are sheared twice a year, so not a breed for the beginner.

**Bagot** An ancient British breed with a striking, long black-and-white coat and an impressive set of large horns. The head and shoulders are black, but everything behind the shoulders is white. A nervous breed, so not recommended for the beginner.

**Boer (Above)** A specialist meat breed from South Africa, it's white with a reddish-brown head, floppy ears and a strong, muscular body. It produces less milk than other breeds, but is still a good dual-purpose choice. Males can weigh as much as 150kg (330lb).

**British Alpine (Above)** Good milkers, British Alpines have predominantly black coats, with white face, legs and tail markings. It has what is described as a 'rangy' build, quite angular in appearance and very impressive when the coat is in good, glossy condition.

**British Saanen (Above)** Probably the most popular milking breed because of its yield and length of lactation. These white goats have an easy-going nature, so are a good choice for beginners. Saanens are often used as foundation stock in commercial farms and cross-bred with other breeds.

**British Toggenburg (Above)** The Toggenburg has similar white markings to the British Alpine, but is predominantly brown. One of the most popular breeds, and a favourite with cheese-makers.

**Golden Guernsey** A golden-coated breed, with some variations in shade and length of coat. Good, quiet temperament, and one of the smaller dairy breeds, so it's easier to handle. There is also a British Guernsey, which is similar, but larger.

**Pygmy goats (Left)** Just like bantams in chicken breeds, these are miniature versions, which make very popular pets. Easy to handle, they are a good choice for children or if you have a limited amount of space and accommodation available. The Pygmy Goat Club stipulates that a male pygmy should be no more than 56cm (22in) at the withers; females are smaller still.

Pigmy goats make popular pets and are easy to handle.

## What about cashmere?

If you have heard people talking of 'cashmere goats' and are wondering why these aren't included in the list of breeds, it's because there is no cashmere breed. Cashmere is the soft, downy layer of insulating hair that grows underneath the main outer coat. Normally, this is moulted in spring, but it can be harvested at other times by combing.

# Pigs

Pigs are often top of the list for newcomers to smallholding, partly because they're such charismatic animals, and partly because they're relatively easy to keep. They are certainly far easier to manage than sheep or goats.

More and more people are enjoying their own home-reared pork these days and, once you have reared your own, you won't go back to the supermarket. The easiest way to enjoy your own pork is to buy in weaners – pigs aged between six and eight weeks old that have been separated from their mother and are eating solid food. Traditional breeds will reach pork weight by five to six months, though fast-growing modern breeds and cross-bred pigs can be ready up to two months earlier. Pigs can, therefore, be the ideal short-term project, giving you home-grown meat within as little as three to four months.

## Registration and identification

As with all the four-legged livestock mentioned so far, your smallholding must be registered before you can take on pigs (see Chapter 3). You will need a herd number, which will be used on ear tags (or slap-marks) on any pigs over 12 months old that leave your holding. When you buy in pigs that are less than 12 months' old, they do not need to be tagged before leaving the vendor's premises – they can move with a temporary identification mark (such as with stock marker spray). They don't need to be tagged with your herd number unless they leave your land.

Pedigree pigs have to be tattooed or notched, according to individual breed society requirements, so seek advice from the appropriate organisation.

When it comes to sending pigs for slaughter, a metal tag must be applied, as plastic management tags will not always withstand the heat used in cleaning the carcass. Alternatively, pigs can be slap-marked, using a long-handled pad of needles covered in ink which leave a kind of tattoo on the skin.

A metal slaughter tag.

**For a complete guide to starting off with pigs, right through to breeding and showing, see the Haynes *Pig Manual*, by Liz Shankland (Haynes Publishing).**

## Movement

Any movement of pigs must be reported using an electronic Animal Movement Licence (eAML2). There used to be a paper document, similar to the AML1 used for sheep, goats and deer, but since 1 April 2012, all movements have had to be recorded electronically, by filling in an online form, which can be accessed through the website www.eaml2.org.uk, or by using a dedicated telephone service (0844 3358400).

The new procedure brought an end to new keepers having to send off part of the old paper form to their local trading standards department, and also removed the need to fill in a separate Food Chain Information form for the Food Standards Agency when taking animals for slaughter. The electronic form combines the two lots of information in one.

The movements of pigs onto your holding imposes a 20-day standstill on all other pigs there, and a six-day standstill on sheep, goats and cattle.

Electrified tape separating groups.

## Accommodation

Organise suitable housing and enclosures beforehand, and ensure that the area where you intend to keep your pigs is up to the challenge of containing these clever animals. Pigs – particularly small ones – are renowned escapologists, and it pays to have good stock fencing with a strand of barbed wire at the bottom.

Electric fencing is a popular choice as a temporary solution, or for strip-grazing. It allows you to move pigs onto fresh ground when the need arises. It's worth training your pigs to respect an electric fence by setting up a test situation in a secure building before installing it in the field.

There are a variety of options when it comes to choosing accommodation for your pigs, but the most popular is the

Michele Baldock

An Iron Age sow with nose-rings.

The Middle White's short nose means it roots less than other breeds.

traditional dome-shaped ark, made from wood and galvanised sheeting. Alternatives include barns or stables, traditional stone pigsties and straw shelters made by layering bales.

## Rooting behaviour

Pigs are excellent for clearing scrub and digging up weeds, but it is surprising how much damage they do to land within a short space of time. Rotating stock helps, but in consistently wet weather the ground has little time to recover. Prepare alternative areas, or even indoor accommodation, just in case you have to move them in really bad weather.

Rooting is an expression of natural behaviour and nothing (apart from nose-ringing, which many smallholders would be reluctant to do) will deter the constant ploughing. You could choose a short-snouted breed that is less likely to destroy the ground.

## First pigs – boars or gilts?

Good breeders will often advise you to start with boar piglets because you won't be tempted to hang on to them in the same way as you might gilts.

Boars grow at a faster rate than gilts, and normally give you a leaner carcass. If you're raising your pigs for pork, they will be off to the abattoir before they become sexually mature, so you need not worry about aggressive behaviour. Fewer and fewer pig breeders are castrating these days, and there are EU plans afoot to outlaw the practice entirely within the next decade.

If your only aim is to produce meat, the sole reason to opt for gilts is if you want to produce bacon, which means keeping pigs for eight to ten months.

## Boar taint

Butchers' tales about boar taint have put many potential pig-keepers off the idea of taking on male weaners. Boar taint is an unpleasant smell and taste, which affects the meat of some male pigs. Most often it's seen in older males from commercial strains that have been reared under intensive conditions. Taint is rare in traditional breeds, possibly because they're slower to mature and aren't fed as intensively.

Boar taint is caused by two compounds in the fat; androsterone and skatole. Androsterone is a steroid, and is produced as the boar reaches puberty. Its function is to act as a sex pheromone, which helps make the female pig receptive. Skatole is produced when the amino acid tryptophan is broken down in the gut. It's found in both male and female pigs, but accumulates more in males. Diet and environment can influence how skatole causes boar taint, and cleanliness has been shown to be a factor in reducing skatole levels.

## Buying pet pigs

Pigs aren't good in human households, so if you're thinking of keeping some as pets, they must be allowed access to the outdoors – at the very least, during the day. Also, pigs are herd animals and need the company of their own kind, so don't just buy one and think it'll be happy with your dog or cat for company.

You have no doubt heard of the so-called micro-pigs favoured by celebrities as fashion accessories. Well, there is no such thing as a micro-pig; it is a phrase coined by canny businesspeople looking for a way to make a quick profit by breeding a runt from one litter to a runt from another.

Eventually the buyers come to their senses: their pigs turn out to be less-than-perfect house guests, ripping up carpets, floorboards and tiles, terrorising pets and children, raiding the food cupboards, and leaving urine and faeces wherever they choose. Although they may be the offspring of two runts from two different litters, thanks to genetic throwbacks, they can grow as big as their ancestors.

One of the things that some people fail to realise when they get their micro-pigs is that they're still pigs as far as the law is concerned, and that means they have to be kept at a registered holding and only moved in accordance with the regulations.

This 'micro-pig' pictured at nine weeks old grew into a full-size boar weighing 127kg (20 stone).

Margaret Smith

A pot-bellied pig that destroyed carpets and floor tiles.

## Feeding

In the wake of the UK foot-and-mouth outbreak of 2001, strict regulations on what could and couldn't be fed to pigs were imposed. The devastating epidemic – which resulted in more than six million animals being slaughtered – was traced back to a farm where pigs had been fed unprocessed waste food. Now no waste food – whether it has passed through a domestic or a commercial kitchen – can be fed to pigs. So forget those stories of how someone's grandparents used to keep a swill bucket under the sink for dinner-plate scrapings. It's no longer allowed.

The easiest way to feed your pigs and ensure they get the nutrients they need is to feed a commercial ration. Pelleted food, sold as pig nuts or rolls, contains cereals with added vitamins and minerals. It's formulated with specific stages of the growing phase in mind from weaner to finishing (slaughter) age.

All young animals need a high level of protein in their food, and the level should be decreased as they grow older if they're being raised for meat. Traditional breeds will reach pork weight in around five to six months' time, but commercial breeds can finish up to two months earlier.

## Supplying water

The importance of water should never be underestimated, particularly with regard to pigs. An adult pig can consume as much as 8 litres (14pt) a day and more than twice that for a sow with piglets. A pig needs to drink twice as much water as it eats food, otherwise the normal salt levels in the body become toxic.

## Health

If you've purchased from a reputable breeder and are not buying in any other stock from markets or unreliable sources, you should have few health worries as you raise your pigs to pork or bacon weight.

**Worming** The weaners you bought should have been wormed at weaning, and should appear fit and healthy when you collect them (see Buying your first livestock, page 70, and Buying at auction, page 70). You shouldn't have to worm them a second time before sending them for slaughter.

**Parasites** Pigs can get external parasites like mange mites and lice, but these are easily treated with injectable drugs that kill both these and any intestinal worms.

## Choosing breeds

**Berkshire** Compact and docile, a popular pig for first-timers. Light-boned, it produces a good ratio of lean meat to fat and can be finished early (around four to five months).

**British Saddleback** One of the most popular and most easily recognised of breeds. There were originally two types of saddleback – the Essex, which came from East Anglia, and the Wessex, which originated from the New Forest in the south of England.

**British Landrace** One of the most popular commercial breeds in the UK and other parts of Europe, renowned for its long, lean carcass. Not good outdoors because of the pale, thin skin and fine coat.

**Duroc** Highly valued in cross-breeding, the Duroc is one of the most widely used for improving carcass conformation. Meat has lots of intramuscular fat ('marbling') which improves succulence. Often difficult to handle, not one for beginners.

**British Lop** The rarest native breed, with approximately 200 registered breeding sows. Often described as the Devon Lop or Cornish Lop. Hardy, but needs protection from the sun. A docile breed, so ideal for beginners.

**Gloucestershire Old Spots** The original orchard pig or cottager's pig, traditionally reared on windfall apples and whey. Folklore says the spots were caused by falling apples. The meat has EU Protected Food Name status, so only meat from pedigree stock can use the breed name.

**Hampshire** Similar to the British Saddleback, but with pricked ears. Fast-growing, long legged, and the sows produce large litters. Meat is lean and muscular. Large, but manageable.

**Large Black** Docile and lop-eared breed, the only completely black pig native to the UK. Its colouring helps it to resist sunburn. Often referred to as the Cornish black. Economical to raise; good grazers which convert foraged food very efficiently.

**Iron Age** A Tamworth x wild boar hybrid, this looks like wild boar but can be kept as any other domestic pigs. Pure wild boar come under the Dangerous Wild Animals Act, 1976, and stringent security measures must be satisfied before a licence is granted (see Wild boar, page 131).

**Large White** One of the founder breeds of the National Pig Breeders' Association, now the British Pig Association. Popular in its own right, but also favoured for cross-breeding, it is used to improve carcass quality. Known in the US as the Yorkshire White.

**Kunekune** Pronounced 'kooney kooney', the name means 'fat and rounded' in Maori. Those in Britain came from New Zealand, but the exact origins are uncertain. Most popular as a pet pig, but it can also be raised for meat.

**Mangalitza** Curly-coated, the Mangalitza is found mainly in Austria, Germany, Hungary, Romania and Switzerland. It contains some traces of an English breed, the Lincolnshire Curly Coat (extinct since the 1970s), because during the 1920s and 1930s hundreds were exported to Austria and Hungary for cross-breeding with the native Mangalitza.

Dan Walker

James Davies

**Middle White** Often described as a 'lovely, ugly pig', this breed has a 'dished' face which is a legacy from cross-breeding with Asian pigs. The patron of the Middle White Pig Breeders' Club is celebrity chef Antony Worrall Thompson.

**Tamworth** The Tamworth was considered a poor choice for cross-breeding when Asian pigs were introduced into many pigs' bloodlines, so it is the purest of the British breeds. Dual-purpose pigs, famed for both pork and bacon, and extremely hardy.

**Vietnamese Pot-bellied** Developed in Vietnam in the 1960s as a dwarf pig, the breed found fame in America as a novelty pet.

Fairly small – around 42cm (16in) tall, they tend to put on fat if not encouraged to exercise.

**Oxford Sandy and Black** Known as the 'plum pudding pig' because of its markings. The colour can be anything from pale sand to deep ginger, with black blotches. Generally docile and hardy, it is a popular choice as a bacon pig.

**Piétrain** This Belgian breed is the most powerfully built of pigs, with huge, double-muscled hams and an extremely lean carcass. Popular for cross-breeding to improve carcass conformation.

**Welsh** The only indigenous Welsh breed, this pig is often confused with the British Lop and the Landrace because of its colouring and lop ears. Economical to raise, it has a long, level body and deep, strong hams.

# Cattle

Unless you have plenty of land, some good outbuildings, some experience with cattle, and lots of time on your hands, this particular species could be a tough one to start with.

When you visit agricultural shows, it's difficult not to be swayed by the sight of handsome Highland cattle with their shaggy coats and long horns, but cows are immensely high-maintenance as far as livestock are concerned. They are demanding in financial, physical, and emotional terms. Some smallholders who already keep them may disagree, but most people who are just dipping a toe into the world of livestock keeping for the first time will find cattle a bit of a stretch.

Another downside to keeping cattle is that there are far more health and movement regulations to obey, and mountains more paperwork and inspections involved. Keeping cattle is an increasingly complex business.

Whether you need cattle to graze your land, would like to have a regular supply of good beef, or merely like the idea of seeing cows in your fields when you look through the window, it might be worth putting the word around and seeing how many farmers come running when they know there's spare grazing space available. Letting out fields for grazing can be a nice little earner if you live in an area where land is scarce. You may be able to choose to be paid in real money or meat, or both. However, be sure to ask around to find out what the going rate for grazing land is before naming a price and shaking hands on a deal.

## Identification and movement

Cattle are more complicated creatures to move than other livestock. Whereas with other animals you will be dealing with your trading standards department, in the case of cattle it's the British Cattle Movement Society. All cattle in the European Union, and in many other countries, are individually identified and their movements traced throughout their lives.

The Department for Environment, Food and Rural Affairs (Defra) is responsible for cattle identification and tracing issues in England; the Scottish Government carries out this role in Scotland; and the Welsh Assembly Government does the same in Wales.

The Rural Payments Agency (RPA), through the British Cattle Movement Service (BCMS), runs Great Britain's Cattle Tracing System (CTS) database on behalf of the English, Scottish and Welsh ministers. In Northern Ireland, information on registration, identification and movement of cattle is maintained by the Department of Agriculture and Rural Development, while in the Republic of Ireland, it is the Department of Agriculture, Food, and the Marine. All cattle-keepers are obliged to abide by similar regulations, so this section will concentrate on procedures in the UK.

In the UK, the main roles of the BCMS are to maintain the CTS database, issue cattle passports, and to process information about cattle births, movements and deaths received from keepers. If you already keep sheep or goats, you have to inform the BCMS that you intend keeping cattle. You must also inform your nearest Animal Health and Veterinary Laboratories Agency (AHVLA office), which will issue you with a herd mark for your cattle. You will need this in order to buy ear tags.

### Cattle Passport
### Pasport Gwartheg

British Cattle Movement Service
Gwasanaeth Symud

Ear tag / Tag clust:
**UK1234567100007**

| | |
|---|---|
| Breed / Brid: | Holstein |
| Sex / Rhyw: | Female |
| Born / Ganwyd: | 04/10/2008 |
| Genetic Dam / Mam Enetig: | CH122112020101 |
| Surrogate Dam / Mam Fenthyg: | CH222011001002 |
| Sire / Tad: | CH111202003001 |

| | |
|---|---|
| Country of origin / Mewnforiwyd o: | Switzerland |
| Date of import / Dyddiad mewnforio: | 06/06/2010 |
| Import health certificate No / Rhif tystysgrif iechyd mewnforio: | CH.2010.0001001 |
| Previous ear tag / Tag clust blaenorol: | CH122112011001 |
| Issue date / Dyddiad cyhoeddi: 15/08/2011 | Version / Fersiwn: 2 |

Please check the details are correct, if not amend and return to BCMS. Gwiriwch fod y manylion yn gywir, os os nad yrlynt galfwch eu haddasu a'u dychwelyd at GSGP.

**Movement history / Hanes Symud**   ** Full movement history held on Cattle Tracing System
** Hanes symudiadau llawn a ddelir ar y System Olrhain Gwartheg

| Location / Lleoliad | Address / Cyfeiriad | Date on / Dyddiad cyrraedd | Date off / Dyddiad ymadael |
|---|---|---|---|
| 01/234/0001 | Farm One, Sample Street, Sample Town | 06/06/2010 | 15/07/2010 |
| 04/234/0004 | Farm Four, Sample Street, Sample Town | 01/08/2010 | 14/10/2010 |
| 05/234/0005 | Farm Five, Sample Street, Sample Town | 14/10/2010 | 29/11/2010 |
| 06/234/0006 | Farm Six, Sample Street, Sample Town | 29/11/2010 | 02/01/2011 |
| 07/234/0007 | Farm Seven, Sample Street, Sample Town | 02/01/2011 | 07/04/2011 |
| 08/234/0008 | Farm Eight, Sample Street, Sample Town | 07/04/2011 | 01/08/2011 |
| 09/234/0009 | Farm Nine, Sample Street, Sample Town | 01/08/2011 | |

**To be completed by keeper on receipt of passport / I'w gwblhau gan geidwad ar dderbyn pasport**

Space for other information

Place your holding address label here
Rhowch label cyfeiriad eich daliad yma

Gofod ar gyfer unrhyw wybodaeth arall

Signature / Llofnod

Date of movement OFF holding / Dyddiad YMADAEL â'r daliad

Signature / Llofnod

**Death details / Manylion y farwolaeth**

Reported electronically tick this box
Wedi'i adrodd yn electronig ticiwch y blwch hwn

Place your holding address label here
Rhowch label cyfeiriad eich daliad yma

Date of DEATH / Dyddiad y FARWOLAETH

Signature / Llofnod

Please remember to return the animal's passport to BCMS within seven days of the animal's death
Cofiwch ddychwelyd pasport yr anifail i GSGP o fewn saith niwrnod o farwolaeth yr anifail

**British Cattle Movement Service**
Gwasanaeth Symud Gwartheg Prydain
Curwen Road, Workington, Cumbria, CA14 2DD
General helpline / Cyffredinol: **0845 050 1234**
Cymraeg: 0845 050 3456
Email / Cyfeiriad e-bost: bcms-enquiries@bcms.rpa.gsi.gov.uk

**Report births, movements and deaths electronically using:**
Adrodd ar enedigaethau, symudiadau ac marwolaethau yn electronig gan ddefnyddio
• CTS Online / SOG Ar-lein: www.bcms.gov.uk
• CTS self service line: 0845 011 1212
  Llinell Hunan Wasanaeth SOG: 0845 011 1213
• Or using a farm software package / Neu'n defnyddio pecyn meddalwedd fferm

**For TSE use only / At ddefnydd TSE yn unig**   **Born /Ganwyd** 04/10/2008   **UK1234567100007**

## Tagging

- Cattle born on or after 15 October 1990 and before 1 April 1995 must be identified with an approved ear tag.
- Cattle born on or after 1 April 1995 but before 1 January 1998 must be identified with an approved tag applied to the right ear which shows the animal's unique alphanumeric (letters and numbers) identification. Each unique identity stays with the animal all its life.
- Cattle born on or after 1 January 1998 must have an approved ear tag in each ear. Both must show the same unique alphanumeric identification.
- Cattle born on or after 1 July 2000 must have an approved ear tag in each ear. Numeric tags were introduced on 1 January 2000 but made compulsory on 1 July 2000. Animals must be double-tagged, and both tags must have the same unique number.

## Registration and passports

All cattle must be registered on the Cattle Tracing System (CTS), and you must apply for a passport within 27 days of birth. Applications can be made online via the CTS website. You will need to supply details about the animal, which include breed, sex, dam (mother) and date of birth.

The passport must be held by the keeper of the animal; if the keeper changes it must be given to the new keeper. Movements of cattle on and off your holding must be reported within three days and you must keep your own records, either in a book or on computer.

There are various types of passport in use – some are single-page documents, some older ones are rather like chequebooks, while others are certificates of registration. If you buy cattle, the type you get will depend on when the animal was registered. Rather like a car log book, the passport shows each keeper of the animal and addresses. Movements have to be recorded on the passport and also reported to the BCMS within three days.

## Testing for bTB

Bovine tuberculosis (bTB) is one of the most difficult health problems currently facing farmers. It is a chronic, infectious disease, which affects the respiratory system and can affect cattle, goats, pigs, badgers and many other mammals, including humans. It can be spread from animal to animal, and also by contact with contaminated equipment, feed, or slurry.

Routine testing of cattle has to be carried out by law. The frequency of tests depends on where you live and the prevalence of bTB in your area. Your herd could be inspected once a year or once every two years – maybe every four years in some areas, where bTB cases are rare. The onus is on the cattle owner to arrange testing by the specified date.

If bTB is suspected in a herd, the case is referred to the AHVLA, which will arrange an inspection, further tests, and impose restrictions on movement of cattle and the sale of unpasturised milk or products made from it until further investigations are carried out. Cattle which are shown to have bTB will be slaughtered and compensation arranged.

## Choosing breeds

If you really want to take on some cattle for the first time, Dexters might be the answer. Smallholders who want a 'house-cow' for milking are often advised to go for Dexters. Jerseys are also frequently suggested, because of their docile nature, smaller milk yield, and particularly rich milk in comparison to other dairy breeds. The downside of Jerseys is that, because they are dairy cows, any calves they have will not have much meat on them, unless crossed with a suitable bull bred for meat rather than milk.

The Dexter is the smallest of the British breeds of cattle – about half the size of a Hereford – and stands around 1m (3ft) high at the shoulder. It's described as a dual-purpose breed, equally capable of providing good milk and good meat. Because of its size (300–350kg/660–770lb), it's considered easier to handle than larger breeds. It comes in three colours, black, red and dun, and there are short-legged and longer-legged types.

Dexters are economical to raise; heifers mature early and can be put to the bull at 15–18 months of age. They're noted for their longevity, too, and, according to the Dexter Cattle Society of Great Britain, have been known to breed for 14 years or more. Average carcass weights range from 145–220kg (320–485lb), with a good meat-to-bone ratio. Dexter meat is popular with people who want small joints, so it sells well at farmers' markets.

Originally from south-west Ireland, Dexters are hardy and good outdoors all year round. Because they are light-footed, they have proved popular right across the UK for use in conservation grazing schemes where heavier cattle would not be suitable.

## Accommodation

Dexters are compact animals, and it's generally accepted that you can accommodate two on the amount of land you would normally devote to one standard-size cow. Most textbooks will tell you that one standard cow requires one acre (0.4ha) of good grazing land, so you could get two Dexters to an acre. This will depend on the quality of the land, the weather and other conditions. If your land gets incredibly boggy, for instance, you're going to have far less good-quality grass available.

You'll need a good field shelter to protect your animals from the elements. Unless your stock fencing is particularly strong, you're also likely to need electric fencing to prevent your cattle from wandering where they shouldn't.

Most commercial farmers take their cattle indoors in October or November, depending on the weather, and often don't turn them back out to grass until April, or even May in

The Welsh black is another breed smallholders might consider, as they are hardy and not too large.

Highland cattle may look magnificent, but they are not for beginners.

Ruth Jones

some places. This protects them from the worst of the weather, helps keep milk yields up in dairy cattle and rests the ground when it is at its most vulnerable; seriously poached ground means next year's grass will be disappointing.

Some Dexter breeders are able to keep their cattle outside all year round, but on a small acreage, this might not be possible. Always ask experienced breeders for advice if you're unsure – don't go ahead and buy your cattle and then end up searching around for additional grazing.

If your cattle will be indoors over winter, make sure you have decent, watertight, well-ventilated and well-lit outbuildings. If in doubt about their suitability, ask a farming neighbour or your vet for advice.

Do not underestimate the work involved in looking after cattle over winter. Remember, their accommodation will need constant mucking out and you're going to be using a huge quantity of straw or other materials for bedding. And, of course, you have feed costs to consider.

## Feeding

Grass is the cheapest food but you'll only be able to rely on it from spring to autumn. The rest of the time you'll need to feed hay or silage – purchased from suppliers or produced on your holding earlier in the year – or provide purpose-made concentrated food.

Michele Baldock

Dexters are a good breed for beginners.

Don't forget the water! A cow can drink about 30 litres (53pt) a day – more in hot weather – so ideally have automatic drinkers set up. Make sure they have access to water when freezing temperatures hit.

## Keeping Dexters for milk

Raising cattle for meat is one thing, but if you want milk as well, you're entering a whole new, complicated world. So far, when talking about the various animals you might consider keeping, this book has avoided talking about breeding because you should get to know how to look after animals before you jump headfirst into the advanced class. This section doesn't suggest anything different, but, if you want a cow for milk, she first needs to calve.

A surprising number of people don't realise that, in order to keep a cow milking, she has to keep giving birth. Confusion may arise because goats are often able to go for

several years between kids without losing their milk. Human mothers, too, can carry on breastfeeding for as long as five years, sometimes more.

It is normal to have one calf a year, so you need to think about where you are going to find a bull, or an artificial insemination (AI) technician. Dexters generally calve fairly easily, but you will still have to know what to do in an emergency, and how to care for the calf once it is born, so get trained up before you even think about buying a cow that's already pregnant, or before you decide to get yours into calf.

When the birth is over, you'll have to wean the calf and get to grips with learning to milk by hand. Your cow is going to need to be milked twice a day, and she will not appreciate it if, one day, you fancy an extra hour or two in bed. Make sure you can cope with the technique of milking and have the required facilities. Just as importantly, line up a relief milker or two, in case you can't do it on occasions.

# Alpacas and llamas

Alpacas clipped and haltered for a show.

More and more smallholders are being seduced into keeping camelids – the group of South American animals that includes llamas, alpacas, camels, guanacos and vicuñas. Alpacas and their larger relatives, llamas, are the most popular in the UK, and it is easy to see why, with their big, doe-like eyes and friendly personalities.

Camelids are popular for a variety of other reasons: they are relatively long-lived (12 to 20-plus years) and make excellent pets; they help graze land effectively; their fleeces produce a fine fibre that can be spun like wool; they guard sheep and poultry from predators; and they can be used as pack animals. Llamas, in particular, are strong and easy to train to pull carts for trekking and other attractions.

As camelids are not reared for food, they aren't subject to the tagging and movement regulations that apply to farmed animals, although you will need a CPH number.

Herd animals by nature, camelids shouldn't be kept alone. You will be hard-pressed to find a reputable breeder who will sell you just one; they should be in groups of two or more, and they're also quite happy sharing a paddock with other livestock. Stocking rates recommended by the British Camelids Association are six to eight alpacas per acre (0.4ha) or four to five llamas per acre, though some breeders suggest fewer. As with all livestock, a lot will depend on the nature of your land and what it can cope with.

**Alpacas** normally command more of an 'aaaahh!' factor than llamas because of their more manageable size and tufted heads. They normally reach 1m (3ft) tall at the shoulder and weigh anything between 45kg and 85kg (99–187lb). There are two types of alpacas, the huacaya and the suri. The kind you are most likely to see in the UK is the huacaya, which is probably the most hardy. They come in a wide range of colours, including all shades of brown, black and grey. The less common suri has a long, soft fleece that resembles dreadlocks.

**Llamas** There are several types of llama, but the kind most frequently seen in the UK is the ccara, which has a short- to medium-length coat. Llamas are generally cheaper to buy than alpacas, but they're larger and take up more space – an adult llama can be as tall as 115cm (45in) and can weigh as much as 160kg (350lb).

## Accommodation

A three-sided field shelter or an open barn for shelter from the rain and sun is normally sufficient for both alpacas and llamas, as they are hardier than they look. Normal stock fencing is usually able to contain them, though some breeders recommend an additional strand of wire on top for llamas – but not barbed wire, as the wool can get caught. Unlike other large animals, alpacas and llamas do not tend to poach the ground, because they have padded feet, rather than hooves. Another bonus is that they're very clean and tidy animals, choosing a few specific sites for dropping dung, which makes clearing up after them a lot easier.

## Feeding

Alpacas and llamas are described as 'semi-ruminants' or 'small ruminants', because they have three-chambered stomachs rather than four like sheep, goats and cattle.

They forage well and will live on grass throughout the year, though you may need to feed hay, especially if grazing is poor in the winter. Alpacas and llamas are natural browsers – like goats, but not as destructive – and enjoy variety in the diet. As their ancestors came from mountainous regions, they're specially adapted to living on poor-quality food, but some breeders feed a specialist supplement to combat any potential deficiencies. Feeding small amounts of such a concentrate can also help with taming and handling.

## Caring for camelids

When compared to other types of domestic livestock, alpacas and llamas need very little in the way of routine maintenance. They do need to be wormed and also vaccinated against clostridial diseases, and their feet need to be trimmed several times a year, depending on the type of land they're kept on. Fortunately, they don't suffer from foot rot, they don't need to have their tails docked, and they rarely suffer from fly strike – although there have been cases reported.

Alpacas generally need to be sheared once a year (suris often every other year), using electric sheep shears. Llamas can be sheared, too, but it is not essential as the fibre can be harvested by combing.

The teeth of both species can become overgrown if they don't get sufficient wear, and may need to be trimmed by a vet using equine dental equipment.

They can pick up intestinal worms, but these are easily treated by injection.

Llamas thrive well outdoors and need minimal healthcare.

# SOMETHING DIFFERENT

You may feel that the usual domestic animals are a bit boring and that you fancy rearing something slightly more unusual – maybe to create a novel niche market.

The face of farming is changing like never before and some traditional farmers are looking towards exotic animals as a way of making a living in increasingly difficult times. However many 'proper' farmers decide to diversify, you can guarantee that the majority of those who take the gamble and try something a little out of the ordinary will be enterprising smallholders.

Whereas the term 'livestock' once meant familiar farmyard animals, there are now people rearing everything from ostriches and rheas to water buffalo and wild boar.

Apart from the standard statutory requirements, some factors to bear in mind are how your neighbours might react to living next door to some exotic beasts, the reliability of your fences and other security measures, and how you might market the meat or other products.

Of course, it should go without saying that you should get some experience with conventional livestock under your belt before venturing into anything too ambitious.

## Ostriches

These have been raised in the UK since the late 1980s. There are more than 30 farms raising these spectacular birds with the end products being incredibly low-fat meat, as well as feathers, oil and leather.

The ostrich may not be able to fly, but it is the world's largest bird, equipped with super-strong legs that can carry it at speeds up to 70kph (43mph). They can reach more than 3m (10ft) tall and weigh more than 180kg (400lb)

Although originally from Africa, ostriches cope well with the British climate, but they do need to be provided with shelter from wind and rain and a dry sleeping area.

The biggest drawback is security. Ostriches are massive, powerful birds, and are not surprisingly among the species listed under the Dangerous Wild Animals Act, 1976. This means anyone who wants to keep them must first apply for a Dangerous Wild Animals Licence from the local authority.

Emus used to be on the list of animals that have to be licensed, but have now been removed.

One of the conditions of the Dangerous Wild Animals Licence is that the animals have to be safely contained, so perimeter fencing must be suitable to prevent birds escaping and to prevent intruders or animals getting in. Fencing has to be a minimum of 1.7m (5ft 6in) high, but 2m (6ft 6in) is recommended for adult birds. Fence posts have to be sunk into concrete or secured in some other way so that they can withstand the impact of an adult bird. Public liability insurance is another thing you will have to get, in case of break-outs.

## Rheas

A relative of the ostrich, rheas have a similar appearance, but are much smaller. They are still a big bird, nevertheless. Standing over 1.5m (5ft) tall, Rhea americana can weigh 25–50kg (55–110lb) and can run at a speed of 55kph (35mph).

For a bird that originated in the grassy plains of South America, the rhea does incredibly well in Britain's unpredictable climate. Although a field shelter is recommended, rheas need no particular protection against the elements, and will often prefer to stay out in all weathers. Hardy and adaptable, they are low-maintenance animals and are gaining favour for many reasons.

Rhea meat is growing slowly in popularity, and has the same great selling point as ostrich meat – it is low fat, low in calories, and tasty – but more people keep them as quirky and endearing pets than choose to eat them. Leather goods can be made from rhea skin and massage creams are produced using oil extracted from fat tissue. The luxurious feathers and impressively large eggs are also marketable.

Unlike many types of livestock, rheas do not need a huge amount of space, nor lush grass; depending on the condition of your land, a pair could live happily on a quarter of an acre (0.1ha) or less of scrubby ground. Although rheas are related to ostriches, they don't require a Dangerous Wild Animals Licence and all the expensive security measures that come with it, so are a lot easier to accommodate.

### Rearing

There are two types of rhea, the American or greater rhea (Rhea americana) – which is the kind you will see in the UK – and the lesser or Darwin's rhea, which is rarer and around 1m (3ft) tall. There are two colours: smoky grey (the most common) and white.

Rhea males take sole responsibility for incubating and raising the chicks. A male will mate with several females and then build a nest – normally a scrape in the ground that he lines with feathers from his abdomen, leaves and grass. His

large size means he can cover up to 60 eggs at a time and, when they are hatched, he will guard his young fiercely for months to come. Even the female rheas that laid the eggs are kept at a distance because they will attack and kill chicks if given the chance.

Females will start laying at two years old, but their eggs are not normally viable until the third year. Around 40 to 60 eggs can be laid in a year, in a season that tends to start around April and can last until September.

Ratites find it hard to incubate naturally in our climate, as successful hatching requires constant conditions. Nests are normally built outdoors, but wet weather often spells disaster for clutches. Consequently, most breeders take fertile eggs from the nest and incubate artificially, which allows control over temperature and humidity. Rhea eggs take anything from 36 to 44 days to hatch. The young cannot generate their own body heat until they are several weeks old, and so need to be kept warm with heat lamps. They also need to be kept safe from predators until they are well grown and able to defend themselves.

## Feeding

All ratites need a relatively high-protein diet, especially chicks. Breeders recommend giving a proprietary ostrich grower ration, which helps strengthen the bones – particularly those in the legs – until they reach about six weeks old. After this stage, layers' pellets combined with cereals such as flaked maize can be given, but rheas will love a regular supply of green vegetables, particularly lettuce and cabbage.

Omnivorous creatures, rheas are browsers rather than grazers, and are particularly fond of broad-leaved plants, including dock leaves, nettles and other weeds. They'll also occasionally eat seeds, roots, fruit, insects and even small animals – so keep the children's pets safely out of their way. Chicks will try and gorge themselves with just about anything – including wood shavings and compost, which can be toxic – so letting young birds roam free and unsupervised in a garden can be risky.

## Buying stock

One slight problem with rheas is that they are virtually impossible to sex until they are around 18 months old. A vet may be prepared to examine the vent and find out, but it will not be a straightforward job and you will almost certainly be charged a fee. Fortunately, male rheas can live quite happily together in a group for most of the year, apart from during the breeding season, when they become territorial and will fight.

A male rhea showing aggression as he protects his offspring.

# Water buffalo

With their massive horns and powerful bodies, water buffalo look rather fierce and intimidating, but the domesticated kind being reared in the UK are, on the whole, docile creatures.

More and more water buffalo are appearing on farms across the UK as demand for their lean meat and low-fat milk increases. They are becoming an increasingly popular conservation tool, particularly on certain nature reserves, where conventional livestock are not appropriate. Several Wildlife Trusts now use them to eat through tough vegetation like gorse and blackthorn in boggy areas where machinery cannot be used. They help to control scrub and also help keep wetlands open for wading birds.

Water buffalo grazing wetlands.

Water buffalo cost about the same as conventional cattle, and are treated just the same in terms of identification, registration, movement and bTB testing. Unlike bison, they don't require a Dangerous Wild Animals Licence, but they do need really good fencing. The big bonus for anyone concerned about costly vets' fees is that they're extremely hardy. They're relatively low-maintenance creatures and don't seem to fall prey to the usual bovine ailments.

Although milk yield is much less than traditional cattle, what is produced is highly sought-after by those with dairy allergies who don't like the taste of goats' milk. Several companies are selling niche market products made from buffalo milk, including yoghurt, ice-cream and, of course, mozzarella cheese. The meat is wonderful, too – lean and tasty, like the best fillet steak, and low in cholesterol.

Montgomeryshire Wildlife Trust

# Wild boar

Wild boar used to be native to the UK until medieval times, when they were hunted to extinction. Although they continued to exist in other parts of Europe, the resurgence of interest in farming them in the UK once again only began in the 1980s, when several herds were imported. Many have escaped since then and have mated with domestic pigs, with the result that there are now numerous small populations living wild.

Pure-bred wild boar are covered by the Dangerous Wild Animals Act, 1976, and you must have a licence from the local authority to keep them. Your premises need to be inspected to make sure a range of conditions – covering everything from housing to security – are satisfied, and you'll need insurance.

However, with hybrids, regulations like identification and movement are the same as for domestic pigs. The most popular cross is wild boar x Tamworth, which is known as the Iron Age pig.

Mating a pure-bred male wild boar with a domestic pig makes economic sense because, while true wild boar only have one litter a year, with four to six boarlets, a female hybrid will mature earlier, farrow twice a year and have bigger litters.

Cross-breeding with a domestic pig also means they reach slaughter weight earlier than the 18 months the wild boar normally takes to grow. They'll also gain better carcass conformation, because wild boar are rather rangy creatures, with little meat on the back end. The drawback is that the more domestic blood that goes in, the more risk there is of

You would need a licence to keep these pure-bred wild boar.

losing the distinctive gamey-flavoured meat, which is so much in demand.

## Management
Even though some feral populations in the UK are becoming less wary of humans, and attacks are rarely heard of, wild boars are dangerous animals, even when handled regularly from an early age. This means getting close to them in the case of an emergency could be difficult, if not impossible. It's unlikely that many vets would be prepared to attempt giving treatment, unless the animal was sedated.

This wild boar hybrid can be kept as a normal domestic pig.

Martin Gould

# THE END OF THE ROAD

When you start off on your journey of raising livestock for the table, the date when you have to take the animals for slaughter seems a long, long way off.

You will, undoubtedly, form something of an attachment to your animals. It wouldn't be natural if you didn't. Some people get more attached than others and end up keeping theirs as pets because they can't bear the thought of turning them into meat.

Whatever you plan to start rearing, you have to think about the end of the process, too. Animals have to be slaughtered humanely and legally. If the meat is for anyone other than yourself, they need to be killed at a licensed abattoir.

Abattoirs are disappearing at an alarming rate, and abattoirs that slaughter poultry for private customers are even rarer. In the days before supermarkets selling cheap, imported food, everyone bought locally raised meat and there were several abattoirs in every town. You may be fortunate enough to find a small, family-run abattoir, which gives a high level of personal service and is happy to deal with smallholders bringing just one or two lambs in.

On the other hand, you may have to deal with bigger operations, which are more used to handling huge consignments from big commercial producers. They will normally take 'private kill' animals, but you will probably have to fit into their schedule, so you will not be able to pick and choose when you want to take them in. Many abattoirs deal with specific species on certain days. You may find you have to book in advance, so don't leave it until the last minute. Work out when your animals are going to reach the weight you want and contact the abattoir in plenty of time.

Restrictions: You also need to check in advance whether your abattoir has any restrictions on what it will or will not kill. For instance, some will not accept cattle with large horns, like Highland cattle or British longhorn. You may also have difficulty finding somewhere willing to take deer, as they need specialist handling facilities, and the same will apply to pure-bred wild boar and any other species covered by the Dangerous Wild Animals Act.

Some slaughterhouses also have personal preferences about certain breeds. You may have problems booking in some rare breed pigs, such as Tamworths or Oxford Sandy and Blacks, because their long, wiry hair is more difficult to remove than the fine white hair on most modern commercial pigs. In some cases, the slaughterman may simply skin your pig because it is easier to do – in which case the joints will not look as good, and you will not get your crackling, either. Pigs are often skinned because they are too large to fit into the scalding bath – the

Before taking on any longhorned animals, make sure you find an abattoir that will slaughter them for you.

tank of boiling water which contains paddles that skim off the hair. It is therefore important to check what maximum – and minimum – weights the abattoir will accept.

**Information:** The Food Standards Agency is the body which licenses and inspects abattoirs and will be able to give you details of premises in your area. It also produces a range of publications advising on food production, safety and the law.

## Preparing for slaughter

- **Withdrawal period:** Before your animals can go into the human food chain, you have to be sure that any drugs they may have been given are completely out of their system. Most veterinary medicines have a withdrawal period – the time between the date the treatment is administered and when the meat can be eaten. Consult your medical records book and make sure the withdrawal period has elapsed.
- **Identification:** Your animals will have to be identified correctly before slaughter, so check they're tagged or slap-marked. In the case of pigs, metal tags must be used to withstand the heat in the scalding process.
- **Paperwork:** Make sure you have completed your paper or online movement documentation.
- **Loading:** Have a few practice runs loading your animals onto your trailer. Familiarise them with the trailer by taking short trips, maybe just around the farm. You could also try feeding them inside the trailer for a few days before they have to go. When the day comes, allow plenty of time to load, and have some spare pairs of hands around.
- **Cleaning:** Your trailer must be thoroughly washed out and disinfected both before you load your animals and after you have offloaded them. Some abattoirs will have washing out facilities on site, but smaller ones will ask you to sign a declaration pledging to clean out your trailer within 24 hours of leaving, or before it is next used – whichever is sooner.
- **Reversing:** If you're lucky, the abattoir will have a one-way-in, one-way-out system, so you can drive straight into the lairage to offload. However, not all will have this facility, and some abattoirs can be very tricky indeed. At smaller places, it's likely you'll have to reverse in, so if you are not confident enough about your reversing skills, arrange a practice run beforehand. Find out when it's likely to be quiet and have a go at manoeuvring at your own speed. It's a lot easier having a go for the first time when you haven't got a queue of people watching you.

## Butchery

Most abattoirs will offer a butchery service, but the quality of the work will vary. Unless you brief the butcher fully, with your exact requirements, you could end up with joints which are too big or not what you want. There are so many ways of butchering various animals, so have a good chat to the abattoir beforehand and supply precise instructions so there is no misunderstanding.

**Packaging** Find out how your meat will be returned to you. You may be offered the choice of having joints film-wrapped on polystyrene trays, vacuum packed, or simply bagged and sealed. Alternatively, you may get everything back loose, in dustbin-sized bags, so make sure you ask. Make it clear if you want any of the offal or the head kept. Lots of places dispose of these items unless specifically asked.

**Home butchery** An alternative is to get the carcasses collected by another butcher – or cut them up yourself. If the meat is for your own consumption, this is straightforward. But if it's to be sold to a third party, the premises where it is cut must be licensed and supervised by the Meat Hygiene Service. However, local authorities can show discretion and allow cutting at unlicensed premises under certain circumstances, for instance where the abattoir does not or will not offer a cutting service. Having said that, each local authority operates in a different way, and some are more helpful than others, so get in touch direct to find out what they will or will not allow.

## Home slaughter

This is the way it used to be done in the old days, and many smallholders still prefer to kill on the farm instead of putting their livestock through the stress of travelling in a trailer to the abattoir, being penned next to strange animals, and experiencing the unnerving sounds and smells of the killing process.

A lot of people worry about the way their animals will be handled and slaughtered once they have unloaded them, and there have been plenty of horror stories in the news and on Internet forums which support their concerns. Hopefully, plans to install CCTV cameras in all abattoirs in future will reach fruition, and will help to ensure that cruelty cannot take place. Disturbing video footage shot by undercover animal activists has already prompted some leading supermarket chains to ask their suppliers to fit cameras in their slaughterhouses.

If you're planning to kill livestock for your own consumption, you must find out how to do it properly. The Humane Slaughter Association is an excellent source of information and produces a range of detailed publications, including books and DVDs, all available by mail order.

## Who can eat what

The regulations surrounding home-killed meat often confuse smallholders. 'Home slaughter' is the slaughter of a livestock animal by its owner on his or her property for personal consumption or consumption by members of the immediate family. This is perfectly legal. However, if the meat is supplied to others, for instance guests staying at bed-and-breakfast accommodation on the same farm, that would be against the law, as it would contravene European food hygiene regulations.

# GROWING FEED FOR LIVESTOCK

## The importance of grassland

You may not have the space, time, equipment, or inclination to grow your own crops to provide fodder and comfortable bedding for your livestock. However, if you do, you might be able to make significant savings compared with buying in supplies.

Most smallholders will steer away from growing cereal crops, preferring to leave the business of growing, mixing and balancing nutrients to the feed company experts, but there is one foodstuff that anyone with livestock will find it in their interest to learn about growing: grass.

Farmers and agricultural college lecturers often say that grass is the most important crop of all, and that makes a lot of sense. Grass can be extremely valuable, but one of the most common mistakes made by newcomers to smallholding is thinking that it is a 'free' food. The truth is that it is far from free, because pastureland has to be properly maintained, fertilised and weeded in order to help keep it healthy and productive. It takes a great deal of time to look after, so that the cost of manpower has to be factored in, too. Pasture management is a year-round job, and skimping on maintenance can lead to big disappointments.

Nettles can spread quickly if not controlled.

Poor grassland means you have to spend more on bought-in fodder.

poorer soil than one as flat as a bowling green – and it may well lose nutrients faster as water drains away.

But all is not lost. You can improve your grassland by working with the soil. Maintaining a good, stable soil structure will help to increase the water-holding capacity and promote root growth. It'll also help to maintain aeration and drainage, make cultivation easier and reduce the risk of erosion. Well-structured soils are essential for grass and crop growth throughout the year. Compaction, smearing and surface-capping of soils lead to reduced air movement, poor drainage, restricted plant root growth and limited uptake of soil and fertiliser nutrients. This, in turn, means a shorter growing season, reduced stock-carrying capacity (the amount of time your animals can spend on a given area), nutrient loss, increased soil erosion and poorer grass growth.

If you are feeling slightly out of your depth at this stage, it would pay to seek professional advice on what to do with your land, and to ask an experienced contractor to help get the land in shape. Depending on what needs doing, they may suggest:

- Ploughing, to create better drainage and break through compacted layers.
- Aerating the top soil, using a spiked roller to break the surface, to allow the soil to 'breathe' and the water to penetrate, so aiding root distribution and nutrient uptake.
- Adding lime or organic matter to improve soil stability and encourage earthworm activity.
- Installing and maintaining drains, because waterlogged soils are more prone to damage.

## Geography and weather

The physical position of your holding and the climate are two uncontrollable aspects with which you have to learn to live. A holding plagued by cold and wet weather and situated in a high, exposed position will not have the best grass. Similarly, a steep, sloping field will have shallower,

## Your year-round guide to grassland management

This is a rough guide to care and maintenance at various times of the year. Your location, climate and other individual circumstances may alter the time of year you do things and necessitate additional tasks.

| TIME OF YEAR | ACTION | WHY? |
|---|---|---|
| **LATE WINTER** | Carry out a soil test to establish pH and other nutrient levels. | |
| | Optimum soil pH for grass growth is 6–6.5. Soil that is too acidic will need an application of lime to correct the pH. Potash, phosphate and nitrogen are also needed for good growth. Deficiencies may mean a compound fertiliser is needed. | |
| | Clear ditches and check land drains for blockages. | Taking action now saves remedial work later on. |
| | Plough if you plan to reseed in the spring. | To create drainage channels and ease compaction. |
| **EARLY SPRING** | Harrow | Harrowing tugs out all the dead grass/thatch so that the soil can receive air, water and nutrients more efficiently. This should be carried out in the early spring, before the grass starts to grow in earnest. |
| | Re-seed if necessary (or maybe delay to late spring, depending on climate). | To cover bare patches or poorly covered areas. |
| | Roll if necessary. | This will repair damage caused by trampling. Roots can more easily make contact with available nutrients. |
| | Apply nitrogen, phosphates or potash fertilisers where necessary (again, may be better left to late spring in some areas). | Results of the soil test will have indicated whether fertilisers are needed. Timing of the application is crucial; conditions need to be right for nutrient uptake, and to prevent nutrients being washed out of the soil by rain. |
| **LATE SPRING/ EARLY SUMMER** | If fields are not being grazed sufficiently, cut with a tractor and topper or a tractor mower and maintain a length of about 5–7cm (2–3in). If the land is grazed sufficiently in April, May and June there may be no need to cut. | Grass at this length can make its own nutrients more efficiently, and is also more resilient against the impact of hooves. |
| | Target invasive weeds like dock, nettles, Japanese knotweed and ragwort. | Removal earlier in the year is easier than waiting until they have become stronger and more established. |
| **SUMMER** | Make hay, haylage, or silage. | Grass will soon be in flower. Cut now before it becomes 'stemmy' and fibrous and, therefore, less palatable and less digestible. Cutting and storing now for winter feed means nutrients are retained. Grass has less nutritional value once it has stopped growing. |
| | If not cutting for hay/silage/haylage, continue mowing or grazing with livestock to keep grass down to 5cm (2in) in length. | Helps stop weeds from flowering and setting seed. |
| **MID/LATE SUMMER** | Take a second cut for hay/silage/haylage if the grass remains sufficiently good. | Provides more over-winter feed. |
| | Re-seed bare patches if necessary. | Prevents weeds taking hold; sometimes conditions are better than if re-seeding earlier in the year. |
| **AUTUMN** | Continue mowing or grazing. | Helps to keep vigorous autumn growth in check. |
| | Carry out field maintenance tasks, e.g. repairing fences, laying hedges. | It's worth completing jobs while the weather is good. |
| **WINTER** | Keep livestock off wet fields and rotate to other fields as necessary. | Minimises the risk of poaching and compaction by livestock and allows grass and ground to recover. Sheep are best kept off wet fields to minimise the risk of fluke, while rotating also reduces risk of foot rot. |

Silage is baled and wrapped before storage.

## Hay, silage and haylage

Feeding livestock over the winter months can be an expensive business, so most farmers choose to keep their costs down by harvesting grasses and cereal crops while they are at their most nutritious and storing them for use when the animals are brought indoors. The main way of doing this is by making hay, silage, or haylage. Clover is commonly grown with grass because it works well mixed with grass silage or maize silage. It also helps the nitrogen content of the soil, reducing the need for fertiliser.

Bring cattle indoors when fields get waterlogged to avoid more damage to the field.

Hay is made from grasses and other crops, which are cut just as they're coming into flower and then dried before being bailed and stored as over-winter feed. The harvested material is allowed to dry so most of the moisture is removed. Moisture-removal is important for the nutritional quality of the hay, but also for safety; if hay is baled from moist grass, the heat produced can be enough to start a fire.

The difficulty, however, is that the success of haymaking is hugely dependent on the weather. The traditional way of making hay is to harvest the grass and then leave it to dry in the fields for several days, turning at least every day before baling and storing. Rain can be disastrous and can ruin a hay crop; mould can develop and toxins form, posing risks to livestock.

The unpredictability of the British weather means that silage has grown in popularity. Silage is a form of conserved grass (or other crop, such as maize), which is made by farmers during the summer months when the grass supply is plentiful and not required for grazing. Grass is cut and left for just a day to wilt (wilting leads to faster fermentation and better-quality silage) and then stored in a silage clamp or pit, or baled and wrapped in plastic, which effectively 'pickles' it. If stored in a silage clamp, it's compressed to remove air by driving a tractor back and forth over it. Then it is sealed with plastic and weighted down with old tyres.

Silage is quite moist, and livestock usually prefer it to hay; it tastes better and the food value is greater. Silage often forms the bulk of the livestock diet during the winter

months. Maize is a popular crop for use as silage because it's nutritious and filling.

Run-off from silage is incredibly damaging to the environment, being 200 times more polluting than untreated sewage, so make sure any leakage does not go anywhere near watercourses.

Haylage is somewhere in the middle between hay and silage. It is wilted rather than dried, to a dry matter content of 55–70%, whereas hay is 85% dry matter. It's baled and wrapped or bagged to exclude air. No moulding occurs in well-made haylage after wrapping, and nutrient losses from haylage are less than those lost from hay during drying, so the end product is more nutritious.

## Other fodder crops

On a small acreage, growing sufficient crops to provide all your animal fodder is probably out of the question, but you may want to attempt growing a few things to supplement your feed bills. Root crops likes swedes, turnips and mangolds are traditional choices, along with legumes such as peas and beans, but the possibilities are endless.

Whatever you decide to grow, you need to think about rotating your crops – a practice which goes back to Roman times, so is tried and tested. Crop rotation is the system of growing a series of different types of crops on the same site – and grazing animals – in consecutive seasons. This way, the build-up of pests and diseases is avoided. Growing in this way improves soil structure, because you're alternating deep and shallow-rooted crops, and also helps prevent soils becoming depleted of soil nutrients, as different crops have different requirements. The ground does not need to lie fallow to regenerate, and can be kept in use with little or no need of artificial fertilisers; even when it's resting, it can still be productive.

Pigs enjoying fodder beet.

# SELLING YOUR PRODUCE

You may have started off on your smallholding with no intention other than to keep your own household fed. However, once you start to develop a surplus, and once friends, neighbours, or work colleagues realise how wonderful your produce is, they will undoubtedly start asking if they can buy some.

Producing food for yourself and selling on to others are, of course, two very different things. For very good reasons, there are numerous rules and regulations surrounding the sale, storage and transport of food products, so make sure you find out what you need to know and act accordingly.

## Health and safety

If you're planning to sell food or drink, you have a lot of homework to do before you can start. Procedures in any business involving consumable products have to be strictly monitored in order to ensure safety. Recent years have seen many cases of illness – some resulting in fatalities – caused by careless practices, and show that no one can be too careful.

Everyone involved in supplying food for sale for human consumption must meet basic hygiene requirements – in all aspects of the business. This covers everything from the premises and facilities used to the training and personal cleanliness of staff.

Before embarking on any food-related venture, talk to the environmental health and trading standards departments at your local authority for advice. Make sure you understand the legislation, what is required of you as a producer and seller of food, and that you can fulfil all the requirements.

In order to prepare and sell food products, you will need to complete at least a basic food hygiene course at your local college, and possibly some more advanced courses, depending on what you have planned. All food businesses should have a Hazard Analysis and Critical Control Points (HACCP) manual. This is a food safety management system that identifies things that might go wrong in your processes, and details the measures you have in place to control or prevent hazards occurring. Staff in contact with food must receive appropriate supervision, and be trained in food hygiene, to enable them to handle food safely.

The Food Standards Agency (FSA) has prepared some excellent documents offering an introduction to the current legislation. These include FSA Guidance on the Requirements of Food Hygiene Legislation and Starting up: Your First Steps to Running a Catering Business, which can be downloaded from the website www.food.gov.uk; there is a vast amount of useful information on this website and the simplest way to find these documents, and information on related topics, is to type the titles into the search box on the home page. For more specific information about the type of business you are planning to run, contact your local authority's environmental health department.

Premises used for storing, preparing, distributing or selling food must be registered with your local authority at least 28 days before opening for business. Food businesses – whether they be shops, market stalls, mobile catering vans, vending machines, or food delivery vans – are subject to the same regulations, and these regulations apply whether you sell the food publicly or privately, for profit or for fundraising.

[PIC – MARKET STALL 2]

## Farmers' markets

The concept of farmers' markets originally came from the USA. In the UK, the city of Bath was the first to embrace the idea, setting one up in 1997. Today there are more than 550 operating throughout the UK, with more than half being members of the National Farmers' Retail & Markets Association (FARMA), the organisation set up to represent producers

selling directly to the public. FARMA certifies farmers' markets in the UK that operate under its guidelines. Certification means they have been independently inspected and meet certain standards – stallholders must be local farmers, growers and food businesses selling their own produce.

Farmers' markets can be run by farmers' co-operatives, local authorities, community groups, or private companies. Regulations vary from one market to another, but most are based on similar criteria:

■ Farmers' markets exist to enable local farmers and producers to sell direct to the public; to give consumers the chance to buy fresh, locally-grown fruit and vegetables, locally-reared meat and home-made products; and to raise public awareness on issues such as genetically modified (GM) foods and the importance of preserving the rural economy.
■ Producers must have grown, raised, baked, processed, or caught all food sold. The term 'producer' includes the stallholder's family and employees when they are directly involved in the business.
■ Stallholders cannot sell products or produce on behalf of, or bought from, any other farm or supplier. This ensures complete traceability.
■ Produce must be from a defined 'local' area. 'Local' is usually taken to mean within 30–50 miles of the market. Producers from further afield may be considered if the produce they are selling cannot be sourced within the

specified 'local' radius. In the case of applications for pitches by producers of similar foods, preference is normally given to the most local producer.

- The origin of the product, including where it was reared and/or processed, should be on all labelling.
- Stallholders must comply with all local and national laws and regulations regarding the production, labelling, display, storage and sale of goods. All producers must comply with the current food hygiene regulations (see the FSA website: www.food.gov.uk).
- Organisers will almost certainly ask to see the producer's public and product liability insurance certificate; producers will generally have £5m worth of cover for each. Public liability insurance protects against claims by a third party injured or damaged as a result of your business, for example if your stall falls down and hurts someone. Product liability insurance protects against claims arising from the actual food you are providing.
- Producers should display trading names clearly on their stalls, together with a contact address.
- By law, prices must be clearly displayed – either on the pack or prominently on the stall. This makes sense from a practical point of view, too. Having to ask for prices is off-putting to customers, and will scare some away.
- Most loose foods (such as fruit and vegetables), must be sold by net weight, using approved metric weighing equipment. If the food is pre-packed, the metric weight must be marked on the pack, but you can also add an imperial weight in a less prominent position. You must have good weighing scales, calibrated for metric weights and approved by your local trading standards officer. Spot-checks of your scales can be made at any time either at the market or at your farm.
- Producers 'adding value' to primary local produce (such as by curing or baking) should use local ingredients wherever possible. Some market organisers specify a minimum percentage of local ingredients to be used.
- Generally, products containing GM products are not permitted to be sold.

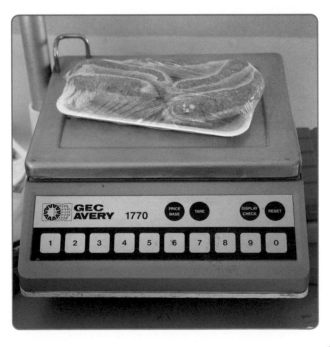

## PROS AND CONS OF FARMERS' MARKETS

### PROS

Farmers' markets can be an excellent showcase for your produce, allowing you to sell quality food at a good price to shoppers who are happy to pay a little more for a premium product. Cutting out the middleman means you (the farmer) get the full retail price – sometimes as much as three times the wholesale price.

It can be very satisfying dealing direct with the public, talking about your produce, your farm and your lifestyle, and collecting feedback from satisfied customers. You don't get that when you hand over your produce to a middleman.

If you sell from your farm gate, customers may turn up sporadically. At farmers' markets, customers all turn up within the space of just a few hours.

Unlike opening a shop, the start-up costs are low. Your biggest outlay (aside from the obvious production costs) will be for renting a pitch and transporting your goods. You can start with just a table to display your wares and invest in something more sophisticated when you start earning money. As most transactions will be in cash, you won't have to wait for cheques to clear.

### CONS

You have to be committed. Satisfied customers will expect to see you every time the market is held, so it's no good deciding that you'd like next Sunday off. You'll disappoint potential repeat customers who might spend their money elsewhere and then stick with the new seller, and you'll also annoy the market organisers. Farmers' markets are not a fair-weather occupation and you'll be expected to turn up regardless of the conditions.

You must be prepared to devote a great deal of time and planning into getting your goods ready for sale. If you're selling fresh meat, rather than frozen, you'll have to ensure that your animals will be ready for slaughter when you need them. This means working backwards to when your animals need to be born or bought in. And you must have a Plan B should you run short of stock, or should your animals not reach the required weight by your projected slaughter time.

Don't forget you also have to allow time for things like butchery, baking, processing, packing and labelling – probably just days before the market. And what happens if you don't sell everything on market day? What would you do with the surplus food? Customers generally prefer fresh produce, so you'll need to decide what to do with your leftover goods.

## Business planning

Draw up a business plan. Work out how much profit you will need to make to support yourself and any partner or family, and how much food per week or month you'll need to produce and sell. Think about your setting-up costs:

- product and public liability insurance
- buying and running a vehicle to transport your goods
- buying, hiring, or building a stall from which to sell
- buying storage facilities, such as a chiller and/or freezer
- buying and/or designing packaging and labelling.

Consider whether you have the time and commitment. Someone has to look after things at home on market day, or while you are preparing for it. What would happen if you or your partner were to fall ill? Who would run the stall?

Explore other ways of selling your produce. It may be that farm gate or mail order and Internet sales would take less time and energy. They may also be more profitable.

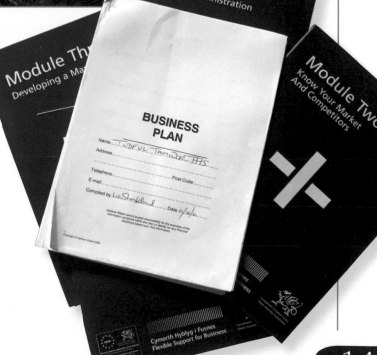

## Secrets of success

If you want to give farmers' markets a try, you need to make sure your stall stands out from all the rest:

- Create an attractive and colourful display that will stop shoppers out browsing. Tell the story behind your produce. Include photographs and information about your livestock and the food preparation process. If you have won any rosettes for your produce or livestock, show them off.

- First impressions are important, so get to the market in plenty of time to start setting up and perfecting your display.
- Make sure all your products are clearly labelled – both to comply with legislation and to make life easier for your customers.
- Smile and be welcoming and think about your appearance. Crisp white overalls or colourful aprons always look smart and professional. Tie your hair back or wear a hat, and make sure hands and nails are clean.

- Engage potential customers in conversation. Tell them about other farmers' markets you attend, offer samples, and give out flyers or business cards.
- It's easy to end up talking to one customer for too long and lose another who is waiting to make a purchase but can't catch your eye. Keep looking around while you're talking and don't be afraid to cut short an unnecessary conversation in a polite and businesslike way.
- Don't undervalue your products. Do plenty of market research beforehand and find out what others supplying similar goods are charging.
- Use the media. Think of news angles to promote your business. Are you the first producer to be selling a certain type of food at your farmers' market? Are you using unusual ingredients or a novel way of processing? Has your business won a grant that has allowed you to boost production? Have you taken on new staff? Have you won an award? Do you have a celebrity customer who loves your wares?
- Persevere! You may not be an instant hit at your first market, and it can take some time before you start building up regular customers who come and seek you out. However, if you stick at it, hang onto the same stall in the same place, and keep providing quality food, chances are you will start to see the same faces coming back time and time again. The proof of the pudding is when new customers arrive saying friends have recommended your produce. That's the kind of thing that makes all the hard work and commitment worthwhile.

# WILDLIFE-FRIENDLY FARMING

**People who know little about agriculture often have a rather blinkered view about the relationship between farmers and the environment, believing there is no way the two can co-exist.**

It is, of course, true that destructive farming practices employed by previous generations did some unforgivable and largely irreparable damage to wildlife habitats. The mechanisation of agriculture got under way in the 1800s, as the advances of the Industrial Revolution brought new inventions like reaping and threshing machines, ploughs and drills.

It took until the 20th century before farmers really started wreaking devastation in the name of efficiency and economy. Ancient woodland and orchards were cleared to make way for wide-open fields to grow crops, or for lucrative forestry plantations. The removal of hedgerows, which had begun in the previous century in order to create bigger fields, continued with a vengeance, giving labour-saving machines like combine harvesters the space they needed to operate. At the same time, government grants encouraged more mechanisation and the use of fertilisers and pesticides to improve production – all at the expense of wildlife.

Happily, times have changed. Financial incentives offered by the European Union, governments, local authorities and other organisations have encouraged modern-day farmers to, once again, become custodians of their land. There is increasing awareness of the need to preserve the wildlife and the landscape that still remains.

A new generation of first-time farmers is growing, too; people who want to make the most of their land, who want to grow crops and raise livestock, but not in ways that have a detrimental effect on nature. More people than ever would like to manage their land in such a way as to benefit wildlife and the environment generally. They may be aiming for some degree of self-sufficiency, or they may have their sights on setting up small-scale commercial enterprises after 'downshifting' from stressful urban jobs. Whatever their plans, they all seem to have one thing in common: they want to do the best they can to give nature a helping hand.

## Reform of the Common Agricultural Policy

From 1962 to 2005 many farmers reaped considerable benefits from the Common Agricultural Policy (CAP) – a subsidy system originally launched in the European Union in order to boost production, guarantee regular food supplies at affordable prices and to ensure a fair standard of living for those in the industry. It was a scheme that rewarded productivity with subsidies.

As environmental awareness grew, the EU decided that, while there was still a need to produce high-quality food and to protect the rural economy, it should not cause damage to the environment, nor to the health and welfare of the animals. Neither should it be disadvantageous to the agricultural industry as a whole.

The Single Payment Scheme (SPS), introduced in 2005, replaced a raft of CAP subsidies which, effectively, had rewarded farmers for keeping large numbers of livestock and for producing food in great quantities. The abandonment of the CAP and the introduction of the SPS removed the incentive to produce more in order to secure subsidies – a process known as 'decoupling'. Rather than being paid in accordance with production, modern day farmers are now given an annual payment based on the size and value of the farm. But there are criteria which have to be met. These include:

- having at least 0.3ha (0.7 acre) of land at their disposal for at least 10 continuous months of the year
- they must be actively farming and/or maintaining the land in good agricultural and environmental condition
- they have to keep up-to-date farm records.

At the heart of the SPS is the idea that landowners must farm in an environmentally friendly way, paying particular attention to controlling pollution, disposing of waste products efficiently, and being careful about the use of pesticides and fertilisers. Every year, a number of farms are chosen for inspection under the 'cross-compliance' regulations and, if a farm is shown not to be complying with any aspect of the rules, the SPS can be reduced or withheld.

There is no obligation on any landowner to register for the SPS, though many consider it beneficial, despite all the form-filling and statutory regulations which have to be taken on board.

## Agri-environment schemes

One clear benefit of the SPS is that it can be a potential stepping stone to other sources of income, such as payments from agri-environment schemes. In order to apply to join any of the various schemes – which reward farmers who volunteer to provide a higher level of care or enhancement of their land – the applicant must first have applied for the SPS.

The stewardship or management schemes on offer vary according to where in UK you live, but the general aims are the same: to encourage landowners to manage their land in a way that benefits the countryside in terms of improving the diversity of wildlife (biodiversity), enhancing the quality of water courses, and protecting the landscape, natural features and historical monuments.

Most governments offer different types of scheme: the first requires a fairly low level of commitment – an agreement to maintain what is already there; the second is for those more willing to bring about beneficial changes through significant improvement works, and who agree to a much stricter list of dos and don'ts.

The good news for the environment is that an increasing number of landowners are realising that joining a scheme makes sound financial sense. The bad news is that the majority of the schemes have become so successful they're over-subscribed. What's more, with government budgets getting tighter, the chances of new entrants being allowed in are becoming slimmer. Still, if you don't ask, you don't get, so find the relevant contact and register your interest (see Further information, page 172).

## Local authority grants

Biodiversity is the buzz-word in conservation circles and restoring biodiversity is one of the biggest challenges facing environmentalists. Each local authority has a Local Biodiversity Action Plan (LBAP) which sets out its plans for protecting and improving priority species and habitats. The officer in charge will be able to tell you whether any grants are available for carrying out conservation work on your holding.

As well as supporting projects that improve areas for nature, grants are sometimes available to those who make their land more accessible to the public. The idea is that visitors are given the opportunity to observe and enjoy their local wildlife, and become more aware of the surrounding countryside. Biodiversity grants are not just for landowners. They can also be given to community groups for small-scale biodiversity projects and are intended to support work that creates or enhances important wildlife habitats or helps to increase the survival chances of key species.

## Becoming nature-friendly

The vast majority of newcomers to smallholding have no desire to farm intensively; few will rely on the holding as their main source of income, which means they may be under less pressure to make every bit of the land 'work' to earn its keep. Even those who do need to make a living out of their holding will probably wish to do it in a way that nurtures rather than damages their surroundings. Whether there are financial incentives on offer or not, it's a fair bet that most smallholders will be want to become more wildlife-friendly.

Whatever your intentions, it's important to recognise that turning your land into your own personal nature reserve may be more complicated than you think. Remember the phrase 'a little knowledge is a dangerous thing'. Lots of new landowners start out with good intentions, but insufficient information. Take, for instance, the example of someone who buys a former dairy farm that is little more than a collection of wide-open pasture fields with hardly a tree in sight. They might think that planting hundreds of native, broad-leaved trees is a great way to help wildlife. This could be the case in some situations, but not if it means creating a plantation that simultaneously destroys a species-rich, wildflower meadow which is already an extremely important habitat for a host of wildlife.

Pond creation is another difficult one. Hiring a mini-digger and excavating a large bowl in a particularly boggy field may seem like a great plan, but not if the field is a prime example of wet grassland – another fast-disappearing farmland habitat.

If you really want to give wildlife a helping hand, the first thing you need is some good advice from a reliable source. The starting point is finding expert help to identify the different habitats you have on your land, and taking advice on what can be done to preserve and enhance them.

Conservation organisations like the Wildlife Trusts are always happy to give general advice, provide literature, and

Chris Wynne

may occasionally even be able to spare a member of staff or volunteer to pop out and take a look at your land, if what you describe sounds like it might already be home to rare species or have potential. It may be that your land adjoins one of their existing reserves or an area known to be frequented by scarce mammals like dormice or water voles – in which case they may wish to survey it and advise on ways in which you can make it even more attractive to such species. Remember that most conservation bodies are charities, and resources are limited, so don't pin your hopes on a load of free advice. It's best to become a member of a local organisation and get involved. That way you'll learn more, get to know the experts and be better placed to ask for guidance.

In some areas, conservation organisations run courses to help introduce new landowners to nature conservation. Decades ago, the work of such bodies was focused on creating nature reserves or other specially protected areas in which wildlife could flourish. But thinking has changed. It's now recognised that, while it's all very well having little 'safe havens' here and there, these oases are of limited value. Wildlife needs to be able to increase in numbers and colonise new areas if it is to exist. If there are no 'green corridors' – effectively, stepping stones of similar habitat along which they can travel – sensitive species can be left stranded and vulnerable on limited patches of land. With no adjacent land available, what would happen if the existing habitat was destroyed – for instance, by fire, disease, development, or some other major change?

If the next-door neighbours happened to be sympathetic landowners who were carefully nurturing similar suitable habitat, there would be a lot more more hope of survival. So, quite simply, your land can play an important part in helping nature conservation – if you know what to do with it.

## Becoming a conservation volunteer

The best way to learn how to help nature is by getting involved with the work of one of the many organisations concerned with protecting and improving the environment – which include the Wildlife Trusts, the Woodland Trust, the British Trust for Conservation Volunteers (BTCV), the National Trust, the Royal Society for the Protection of Birds (RSPB), and many others. Most bodies in the conservation sector rely heavily on volunteers to carry out essential maintenance work on nature reserves, so you will normally get the chance to learn traditional countryside management skills like hedgelaying and drystone walling as well as other useful techniques, which might include using a chainsaw and felling trees.

## Starting points for wildlife-friendly farming

- Get yourself some professional advice on caring for your land. Don't do anything major or irreversible until you know exactly what wildlife and habitats you have and how to deal with them. For instance, you need to be sure you're not destroying a valuable existing habitat before you plant any trees. Similarly, don't fertilise old meadows or drain wet grasslands before checking what wildlife those areas might be supporting.

- Try to provide a variety of habitats, such as wetlands, old grasslands, heath and woodland. If you have space, make the effort to maintain a good mix of crops and livestock. The habitats your land will support will depend on the ground condition, topography, climate and other factors, so be realistic about what can be created.

- Try to minimise the use of fertilisers, pesticides, and herbicides. Keep chemicals and manure away from watercourses. Organic farming, with no application of chemical fertilisers, is usually best for wildlife.

This field may look untidy, but it will be home to countless special wildlife.

**Preserve flower-rich pastures** Take advice before re-seeding pastures, to ensure you're not damaging ancient flower-rich grasslands.

**Use traditional management methods** Grazing is the best way of managing your land – preferably using both cattle and sheep, as they graze in different, but complementary ways. If grazing isn't possible, cutting is the next best option.

**Encourage wildflowers** If you already have fields of wildlife-poor grassland, which have been intensively managed, consider whether you want to set off on the long course of restoring them to species richness. Specialist advice is essential. Fertilising needs to stop, and the land needs cutting or grazing regularly to help reduce the artificially high fertility in the soil. Wildflower species may return on their own as fertility decreases, or wildflower seed can be sown.

**Fringe benefits** If you need to keep your improved grassland as productive as possible to provide fodder for livestock, there are still things you can do to help wildlife. Leave field margins or corners unfertilised and ungrazed or uncut to produce a fringe of rough areas around your more productive grassland. This will help support a greater diversity of plants, more invertebrates, small mammals, and their predators.

**Allow crop stubble to remain over winter**, as it provides a useful source of food for many birds and small mammals. Delay any spraying with pesticides until as near to cultivation as possible.

**Don't remove ivy from walls and mature trees**, as it is a source of nectar and fruit for insects and birds late in the year when other food sources are scarce. It is also useful for roosting and nesting birds and hibernating mammals.

**If you have any really old trees, look after them**, as they can be home to many types of wildlife. Leave standing and fallen dead trees to provide habitat for fungi, insects and birds.

**Provide habitats for bats and birds** Make sure that bats, as well as birds, such as barn owls, swallows, swifts and house martins, can get access to your farm buildings, whether they're old ones or newly-built. Put up nest boxes – different types for different species – where you can.

**Don't lay or cut all your hedges every year**, because bushy hedgerows are a rich source of food and nesting material for birds and mammals. When planting new hedges, always use a mix of native and – if possible – locally grown trees and shrubs.

**Look after existing ponds** Take professional advice before making any new ponds, because it might not be the best course of action to help wildlife.

**Conserve areas of wet grassland** and marsh to help waders and wetland plants.

## TOP TIP

### CREATE WILDLIFE CORRIDORS

You can maintain links between habitats by looking after your hedges and allowing grassy margins to flourish. Don't be too tidy, because overgrown areas provide both food and shelter. Try to allow rough growth alongside streams and rivers to protect wildlife from run-off from things like fertiliser and pesticides. Thick scrub or holes around the roots of secluded stream-side trees could even provide a resting place for a passing otter.

# SHOWING

**Showing livestock is not for everyone, but many thousands of livestock keepers who have pedigree stock agree it's an immensely enjoyable pastime.**

Plucking up the courage to enter a show and parade your animals before crowds of people can take some doing and, once you've done it, you'll either love it or hate it. Those to whom showing is a passion have no doubt about the benefits. Forget about the prize money, it's the personal pride that comes with winning. If you're thinking of becoming a breeder of pedigree animals, shows are the best possible shop window for your stock.

Agricultural events are packed with potential customers, many of whom visit in order to seek out the best stock. There will be many more people who are just browsing, trying to make up their minds about what to choose, and meeting a friendly owner face-to-face who is willing to talk about their particular breed can often be the deciding factor.

No matter what eye-catching display material you have surrounding your animals' pens in the livestock sheds, the best possible advertisement for your herd or flock is a bunch of red rosettes – or, even better, a championship one. Prizes count for a lot, giving the official stamp of approval to your business, and often levering up the prices in the process.

## Getting started

Keeping and showing livestock is becoming a fashionable pastime for a growing number of people from incredibly diverse backgrounds. A great many competitors are full-time farmers whose parents and grandparents have been showing for decades, but there are probably just as many smallholders who keep only a few animals and treat showing as a hobby.

To outsiders, agricultural shows may give the impression of being rather male-dominated arenas, but nothing is further from the truth. The number of women taking part is equal to that of men, if not more in some competitions, particularly in goat, pig and sheep classes.

What keeps most exhibitors going back year after year is not the thought of winning, but the sheer enjoyment of taking part and, above all, the social side of showing. Yes, competing can be a serious business, but it's also great fun. Showing gives you the opportunity to make acquaintances from far and wide. Your new best friends might live hundreds of miles away, or they could even turn out to be living in the next village from you. What matters is that when you meet at each event, the friendship is rekindled and you have a great time.

Breeders come from all parts of the UK to compete in the top shows, often travelling hundreds of miles, spending several hours on the road, and sleeping in their trailers for the duration of the event. A lot of the same faces appear at many of the shows, so it will not take long for you to get to know the 'show crowd' for your particular species or breed.

Established showmen and women are always pleased to see newcomers arriving. The future success of competitions depends on new people being encouraged into the fold, replacing those who retire.

Whatever you are showing, you can be sure that, if you ask for help, you'll get it. Stockmen and women are nice people. One thing they all have in common is that they enjoy letting their hair down at the end of a busy day. You'll find that the best shows will have a 'stockmen's supper' to which

There's plenty of time for socialising after the show.

all exhibitors are invited. This may be free, thanks to sponsorship by a supplier, or it may be subsidised by the show society. If there isn't an official meal, there will be parties in the livestock sheds after the public have gone.

You can take the whole family along to a show, even if they are not all into exhibiting stock. Agricultural shows have woken up to the fact that they need to be all things to all visitors, so various kind of attractions are pulled in to satisfy all tastes.

### Who can show?

One good thing about agricultural shows is that whoever you are and however much (or little) experience you have with livestock, you can enter any event you fancy. In contrast to the pedigree pet world, there's no need to qualify at a small show in order to win the right to exhibit at a major show. Shows are open to anyone and everyone, provided their animals meet the specified criteria.

You may feel more comfortable cutting your teeth at a small village show, where there is often a much more informal atmosphere, but there is no reason why you shouldn't jump in at the deep end. After all, if you have good animals, why not show them off? It doesn't matter whether you've bred them yourself or bought them in – all that matters is that they're yours and you can take them wherever you like.

If you have children – depending on the age restrictions laid down by individual shows – you could get them involved, too. All shows have young handler competitions, which are a great place for youngsters to start.

### Finding a show

Your breed society will have a calendar of forthcoming shows, so note the dates of those that appeal to you and find out when entries have to be in. Entry schedules are sent out months in advance and have to be returned, with payment, long before the actual date of the show. Forms will need to be completed with details of your animals and their pedigrees, and you need to book pens for them as well.

### Accommodation

Sometimes shows offer accommodation for exhibitors in basic, bunk-house blocks, though most people opt for camping on site. Caravans and motor homes are popular, but by far the most frequent sight is that of show people using their rinsed-out livestock trailers as makeshift lodgings. Some become masters at setting up camp in what is commonly known on the show circuit as the Ifor Williams Hotel (Ifor Williams being one of the leading manufacturers of livestock trailers in the UK). Large trailers are used not only for sleeping, but also to house field kitchens capable of cooking three-course meals for large groups of people, and 'lounge' areas where everyone can chill out after a long day in the show ring.

Setting up camp for the night in a trailer covered with a tarpaulin.

There are many drawbacks to sleeping in your trailer – not least the smell of the livestock that used it before you, the rain that drips in through ventilation slots (even when you drape a tarpaulin over the top), and the unyielding coldness of a galvanised metal floor doubling as a mattress. However, compared to paying out for a caravan pitch, and taking two vehicles – one to tow the caravan and another to tow the livestock – roughing it for a few days makes perfect sense.

Take plenty of food and drink with you, because many show sites are way out of town. A few will have shops where you can buy basic goods, but you will probably have to pay a premium.

## Shows and movement regulations

Remember that, if you plan to visit shows, when you return, your livestock will be put on standstill (apart from those going to the abattoir) unless you have an approved isolation unit they can use (see Chapter 6). Similarly, if you are buying new stock or hiring in stud males, make sure you allow good time so that the standstill is over before you plan to take your own animals to the show.

## What can you show?

Forward planning is the key. Experienced breeders carefully plan their births to suit the various age classes, so it pays to find out what those classes are and to think ahead. Animals are normally judged by breed first, with classes for those born within specified periods. The winners of each age class in each breed or category compete for the championship, and then the ultimate winners go head-to-head to battle it out for the supreme championship.

Understanding the age categories is essential if you want to enter an animal. It must fit within a specific category, and to be in with a good chance of winning, it should have been born as close to the 'start date' of the age group as possible. For example, if the age category says, 'Born on or after January 1, 2012', an animal born in May 2012 would look small and insignificant compared to a New Year arrival also in the ring. Regardless of what people say, size does matter when it comes to judging.

Birth dates are not as crucial with older animals, though when it comes to judging females that have reached breeding age, prizes tend to go to those who are further on in pregnancy – blooming, if you like. With this in mind, experienced breeders plan to get their animals pregnant a few months before a show, so they look at their best.

## Choosing stock to show

Only animals with the best features should be bred from, and you'll need to consult the checklist of desired qualities specified in each breed standard. Find your breed society's website or handbook and check the criteria. You should be able to find the points that a show judge will be looking for; each animal will be marked against this list.

If you are fortunate to have a few animals that meet the requirements, and all look equally good, spend time watching them. One will normally catch your eye because it has a certain presence, holds him or herself well, or walks well. Make sure the backs are straight and even; see if they walk with 'one leg at each corner'. Ask for a second opinion from an experienced breeder if you are unsure.

## Preparing for a show

- Ensure that all vaccinations are up to date, because, from a health point of view, shows can be risky places to take unprotected animals.
- Ensure animals are in the peak of health and looking good.
- Check that tags and tattoos are intact. Plastic tags can often get ripped out, while tattoos can fade or become illegible. If tags are missing or illegible, animals can be disqualified.

## First impressions count

Presentation is important, and it obviously helps your chances if your animals are clean and well groomed. This, however, might be easier said than done if they live outdoors all year round. Some serious exhibitors will keep their show pigs, for instance, indoors permanently. Others take their pigs into a barn for preparation a few weeks before an event so that they can be washed and kept as clean as possible. And then there are others who will load their pigs straight from the field into the trailer and wash them when they get to the show.

There are always washing facilities at shows, but the standard of the wash pens varies. Some shows have strong, purpose-built, permanent shower cubicles, with hot and cold water on tap; other shows have temporary outdoor pens made from galvanised hurdles and you'll have to go and get your own water in a bucket.

You must be comfortable handling your animals, and you don't want to stress them out with a new experience just before a show. Practise handling, washing and grooming at home, long before the show season.

A well-presented exhibit can catch the judge's eye.

## Show-ring practice

It helps if you can have a trial run or two in the privacy of your own paddocks before you have to do it in public. Sheep hurdles, cable-tied together for extra strength, will create a makeshift show ring. Whether you're trying to get a sheep, goat, or cow used to walking with a halter, or attempting to get a pig used to a board and stick, working in a confined space with few distractions will help.

## Setting off for a show

Check that your trailer is safe and roadworthy. Bear in mind the transportation regulations mentioned in Chapter 3. If you're going to be travelling more than 65km (40 miles) or for longer than eight hours, you'll need a Transporter Authorisation and a Certificate of Competence. Copies of these must be carried with you.

## What to take with you

There are items you need to make life easier during the show:

- Kit box: A sturdy, wooden box or a plastic toolbox on wheels. This is the place to put all your odds and ends, and it will also double-up as a seat in the kit pen.
- First aid kit for the animals and for yourself: The show will have its own vets on call, should your animals fall seriously ill, but ask your own vet for advice on what you should take with you for minor problems.

- Food, drink and bedding for the animals: Remember to take food and drink containers, plus sufficient feed for the duration of the show. Depending on the show, you may also need to take your own straw for bedding, so check with the organisers beforehand.
- Food and drink for yourself: There can be a lot of hanging around, so it's best to be prepared. You might not be able to leave the livestock building to get something to eat, so make sure you have something at hand.
- Washing kit for the final wash and brush-up, along with wellies and waterproof clothing or a big apron.
- Shovel and brush, for cleaning out the pens each day.
- Mini tool kit – including staple gun, hammer, string and cable ties, for putting up an informative display about your herd – and any rosettes, of course.
- Business cards and flyers to advertise your stock.
- Notebook and pens for contact details of potential buyers.
- Exhibitor's coat and handling equipment, such as a halter, board and stick.
- Small bulldog clips to attach your exhibitor number to the pocket of your coat.

## At the showground

**Documentation** Your movement documentation will be checked on entry to the showground, or by the stewards in your particular section.

**Arrival** You should have been sent a plan of the showground when you received confirmation of you entries but, if not, there will be stewards to direct you. Be aware that the later you arrive, the busier it will be, so if you are not too confident reversing a trailer, plan to get there in plenty of time.

**Off-loading** Stewards will tell you where to back up and off-load. Be patient – you may have had a tough morning loading your animals and battling through traffic, but the steward may have been there for several hours by the time you arrive. Stewards volunteer to help, so be pleasant to them. It pays to build up a good relationship, just in case you need to call in any favours.

You will be shown where to put your animals and your kit. Normally this has to be done quickly, because there will be someone behind you who needs to do the same. Don't worry about your kit – just drop it off and make sure the animals have bedding and water. You can sort everything out later. **Washing out** After off-loading, you'll be sent to wash out your trailer. There will be a designated area for doing this and, at bigger shows, there may be staff to do it for you.

## Entering the ring

One of the most frustrating things about showing livestock is finding out what time you'll be in the ring. Catalogues always give a start time, but inevitably delays happen and schedules slip. You have to be prepared for a great deal of hanging around, but don't be tempted to wander off – you might miss your class.

Be aware of what is happening in the rings. Sometimes show PA systems only extend to the ring itself and not to the livestock building where your animals are housed, so you may miss the commentary if you're not in the right place. Make sure you know what time judging starts and make a note of your class number. Everything depends on the number of entries and how thorough the judge wants to be. Use the time to give your animals a final wash and brush-up, but make sure there's someone who will let you know when you're on.

## Show-ring etiquette

**Dress code** Exhibitors should always be smartly dressed. A white coat with a shirt and tie and proper trousers (not jeans) are the standard dress of good showmen and women. Jeans, combat trousers and wellies are not acceptable, but some people don't seem to care what they wear. If dressed according to the etiquette, it shows that you're taking things seriously and have respect for the proceedings. Without doubt, the judge will be dressed up – men in suits and bowlers, women in posh dresses and hats which wouldn't look out of place at a Buckingham Palace garden party – so you should make the effort.

When your class is called, the stewards should clear the public out of the way so that exhibitors can get their animals safely into the ring. Efficiency varies from show to show, so be prepared to weave through people, prams and even dogs at the less safety-conscious events.

**Keep an eye on the judge** When he or she comes your way, you need to present your animal as best you can. Keep it between you and the judge and try to keep it steady so it can be examined. The judge will want to look at conformation, examine underneath and, above all, see if it meets all the criteria set down in the breed standard. You will probably be asked a few questions, and the more knowledgeable you are, the better. If someone else is showing for you, make sure they are briefed on things like age and stage of pregnancy.

Judges will always be smartly dressed – and so should you be.

**The end result** Whatever happens at the end of a show, if you get a rosette, remember to shake the judge's hand and thank him or her. Always ask for feedback if you don't win anything, as it is useful to know how to improve next time round.

The way you get your animal to stand in the ring can help to show off its best features.

# GLOSSARY

**ad lib feeding** Allowing free access to food at all times.

**Animal Movement Licence (AML)** Required for any movements of sheep, goats, pigs, camelids, etc.

**annual crops** Plants which complete their life cycle within a year or less.

**ark/arc** Outdoor pig house, normally made of a wood frame and galvanised metal sheets.

**artificial insemination (AI)** Method of inserting semen into an animal using a catheter instead of mating naturally.

**back fat** Layer of fat along the back which helps gauge the leanness of the carcass.

**bacon** Cured pork.

**bacon pig/baconer** Pig being reared for bacon rather than pork, and which will be slaughtered between 80kg (176lb) and 100kg (220lb).

**bale** Quantity of hay, straw, or grass compressed into round or rectangular shapes and secured with string or mesh.

**bantam** Miniature breed of chicken, often a quarter the size of the original. Some bantams are 'true' bantams, i.e. there is no large equivalent.

**beeswax** A hydrocarbon produced from the glands on the underside of the abdomen of the worker bee.

**billhook** Hand tool used in hedge-laying.

**biodiversity** Literally, ' biological diversity' – the wide variety of plant and animal life which exists.

**boar** Uncastrated male pig.

**boar taint** Unpleasant odour or flavour in meat from some mature male pigs.

**break crop** In rotational systems, a crop grown to help avoid build-up of disease, and also to add organic matter to the soil.

**broiler** Bird bred for meat.

**Broker, broken-mouthed** Ageing ewe with worn or missing teeth.

**brooding** Process by which the hen incubates eggs by sitting on them. Broody is used to describe a bird intent on nesting.

**bull** An entire (uncastrated) male of breeding age, usually over a year old.

**bullock** Mature castrated male destined for meat production.

**calf** Young bovine animal less than a year old.

**camelid** South American animals, including llamas, alpacas, camels, guanacos and vicuñas.

**candling** Checking the development of an embryo by lighting an egg from behind.

**capon** Castrated cock bird, raised for meat.

**carcass** Body of an animal following slaughter and removal of internal organs.

**chick crumbs** Fine chicken feed with a high protein content to promote early growth.

**chilver** Young ewe which has not yet produced a lamb. See also 'gimmer'.

**clamp** Area used to contain a large amount of compressed winter fodder, e.g. silage.

**cock** Male bird

**cockerel** Male chicken under a year old.

**colostrum** First milk produced after farrowing, rich in nutrients and antibodies.

**combine, combine harvester** Large machine used in harvesting that can separate seeds from stalks.

**Common Agricultural Policy (CAP)** in the European Union, a system of agricultural subsidies and schemes.

**condition-scoring** Examining an animal to check its growth and suitability for breeding or slaughter.

**conformation** Thickness of muscle and fat in relation to the size of an animal's skeleton, i.e. the 'shape' of the carcass profile and degree of muscularity.

**coppicing** Cutting back trees to ground level to create multi-stemmed plants.

**creep area** Separate section of the birthing pen where offspring can feed.

**creep feed** Small, high-protein pellets specially formulated for young stock.

**cross-compliance** Set of conditions which have to be met by anyone claiming payments under the Common Agricultural Policy (CAP).

**crutching, dagging** Removing soiled wool from a sheep's rear end.

**culls** Animals sent for slaughter which are no longer needed because of age, lack of productivity, or condition.

**cultivator** Spiked implement used to break up the soil.

**dairy cow** Lean breed or hybrid, bred specifically for milk production.

**dam** Female parent of an animal.

**dead weight** Weight of a pig carcass once slaughtered and eviscerated.

**Defra** In England, the Department of the Environment, Food and Rural Affairs.

**dished** Used to describe the face of a pig with an upturned snout, such as a Tamworth or Berkshire.

**draft ewe** One which is too old for the rough conditions of hill grazing, but can still be bred from on lower-lying land.

**drenching** Giving medicine by oral means.

**dressing** Preparing the carcass ready for butchery.

**drone male** Bee which mates with a virgin queen.

**dry expression** Used to describe an animal which is neither pregnant nor lactating.

**easement** Right to cross or use someone else's land for a specified purpose.

**embryo transfer** Specialist reproduction technique used extensively in cattle.

**entire** Uncastrated and therefore capable of reproduction.

**erysipelas** Potentially fatal disease, most commonly seen in pigs, which invades the bloodstream, causing septicaemia.

**evisceration** Removal of internal organs; disembowelment.

**ewe** Mature female sheep.

**farrowing** Process of giving birth.

**fat stock/finished stock** Animals ready for slaughter.

**fecundity** Reproductive success of a female, e.g. number born alive/weaned.

**flight feathers** Also known as primary feathers, the first ten wing feathers.

**flushing** Increasing the amount of nutrition given prior to mating to improve fertility. In embryo transfer in cattle, a technique used to harvest fertilised embryos for implantation in surrogate cows.

**fly-strike** Condition caused by maggots eating into the flesh of the sheep after hatching from eggs laid in the fleece.

**foot rot** Infectious, contagious disease of sheep and goats which can cause lameness.

**fostering** Transferring a young animal to a different mother for rearing, e.g. in the case of orphans or multiple births.

**freemartin** Infertile heifer calf born with a male twin.

**fungicides** Chemicals used to destroy fungal diseases in plants.

**gestation** Length of pregnancy.

**gilt** Female pig which has not yet produced a litter.

**gimmer** Young ewe which has not yet produced a lamb.

**ham** Cured pork, normally from the back legs.

**harrow** Tractor implement which helps level the soil and pull out thatch.

**hay** Mixture of grasses, cut just as they are coming into flower, then dried and baled.

**haylage** Grass which is cut like hay, but baled when the moisture content is relatively high.

**heifer** Young female cow up to birth of her first calf or in lactation following the first calving.

**hen** Female bird over a year old, normally past its first moult.

**herbicides** Chemicals used to kill unwanted plant growth.

**hive** Man-made home for bees.

**hog** Castrated male pig, also known as a castrate.

**hogg, hogget** Castrated male sheep between ten months and two years old.

**hogging** In female pigs, showing signs of being in season.

**holding number** A unique number which identifies an agricultural holding.

**honey** Concentrated form of nectar with a long shelf life.

**humus** Organic matter formed through decomposition of leaves and other plant materials by micro-organisms.

**hybrid** Cross-breed designed for optimum performance by selecting desirable traits in parents.

**in calf, in kid, in lamb, in pig** Pregnant.

**incubator** A machine designed to artificially hatch eggs.

**isolation unit** Dedicated place, approved by the Animal Health department, where livestock can be quarantined to avoid the statutory 'standstill' movement restrictions, e.g. for animals travelling to and from shows, and for stud animals.

**killing-out** Percentage (KO%) the weight of the eviscerated or dressed carcass as a proportion of the live weight of the animal before slaughter.

**lactation** Period during which a female animal produces milk.

**lairage** Area in an abattoir where animals are held before slaughter.

**lamb** Young sheep, up to a year old (ram lamb; ewe lamb).

**leaching** Loss of water-soluble minerals from soil.

**legume** Plant which bears pods, e.g. peas or beans.

**line breeding** Process of breeding closely related animals to continue certain favoured characteristics.

**litter** Group of piglets or other animals; dry bedding, such as wood shavings, straw, or shredded paper.

**live weight** Total weight of the animal before slaughter.

**lot** Item, animal, or group of animals, being auctioned.

**maiden** Sexually mature female which has not yet been mated.

**marbling** Visible deposits of intra-muscular fat (fat found within the muscles).

**mash** Powdered livestock feed, usually mixed with water.

**mis-mothering** Particularly in sheep, when a pregnant animal takes another's offspring.

**mole plough** Tractor attachment used to improve drainage which digs deep into the soil to leave channels similar to mole runs.

**moulting** Process by which feathers or hairs are shed and replaced.

**mule** Cross-bred sheep sired by a blue-faced Leicester ram.

**mutton** Meat of older sheep, generally over two years' old.

**nectar** Sugary plant secretion which attracts insects for the purpose of pollination.

**oestrus (heat)** Ovulation period which determines when mating can take place.

**organic matter** Plant or animal residue which has started to decompose.

**pesticide** Generic term for herbicides, fungicides, insecticides.

**piglet** Young pig.

**pleaching** In hedge-laying, interweaving branches to create a dense barrier.

**plough** Tractor attachment which turns over the soil, preparing the ground for planting.

**point of lay** Time when birds begin to produce eggs, normally 16–20 weeks.

**pollarding** Lopping off the top branches of a tree to stimulate new growth and prolong life.

**polled** Used to describe breeds in which horns do not occur.

**pork** Fresh, uncured pig meat.

**porker** Pig reared to pork weight (normally around 60kg/132lb), slaughtered around five to seven months' old.

**poult** Young turkey.

**primary feathers** First ten wing or flight feathers.

**progeny** Offspring.

**prolificacy** Productiveness of a female in terms of healthy offspring per lambing, litter.

**PTO** Power take-off in tractors. The PTO system runs a range of attachments.

**pullet** Female bird under a year old.

**putrification** Decomposition of organic matter.

**raddle** Harness fitted to a ram before mating. It has a pad of coloured dye which rubs off on the ewes' backs, indicating which have been served.

**ram** Mature, 'entire' male.

**roller** Used for compacting the soil.

**rotovator** Used to break down the soil into a fine tilth, ready for planting.

**scours, scouring** Diarrhoea.

**shearling, yearling** Sheep which has been sheared (or shorn) once.

**silage** Grass which has been cut, compressed and partly fermented; used as winter fodder.

**sire** Male parent of an animal (noun); to father offspring (verb).

**slapmark** Indelible identification stamp imprinted on the back of an animal before slaughter.

**sow** Female pig after her first litter.

**stag** Male turkey. Americans prefer the word 'tom'.

**standstill** Following the arrival of new livestock on a farm, the amount of time animals are required to stay put before moving to a new location.

**steer** Castrated bull calf over a year old.

**store** Animal being fattened for meat.

**straw** Dried stalks of cereal crops.

**stubble** Short stalks left in a field following the harvest of a cereal crop.

**suckling pig** Young (often two to three weeks' old) piglet which is taken from its mother before weaning. Cooked whole, this is a delicacy in many parts of the world.

**swill** Mixture of waste human food which is now illegal to feed to pigs.

**swine** American collective name for pigs.

**teaser** Vasectomised male put into a field with females to bring them into season before the fertile male is introduced.

**tegg** Castrated male sheep between ten months and two years old.

**terminal sire** In cross-breeding, a male chosen specifically to pass on particular traits.

**tilth** Physical condition of cultivated soil.

**top-dressing** Spreading fertiliser on the soil.

**tup** Ram kept for breeding

**tupping** Mating.

**underline** In pigs, the double row of nipples.

**weaning** Separating an animal from its mother.

**wether** Castrated male, normally grown on for meat.

**withdrawal period** Legally defined length of time between the final dose of veterinary medicine being administered and the meat of an animal being allowed to be slaughtered in order to enter the food chain.

**yearling** Animal in its second year.

**zoonosis** Disease which can be transmitted between animals and humans.

# FURTHER INFORMATION

## Useful contacts

### GOVERNMENT CONTACTS

**England:**

**Department for Environment, Food and Rural Affairs** (DEFRA) Tel 08459 33 55 77
www.defra.gov.uk

**Rural Payments Agency** Tel. 0845 603 7777
www.rpa.gov.uk

### Scotland:

**Scottish Government**
Tel 08457 741 741 or 0131 556 8400
www.scotland.gov.uk

**Scottish Rural Payment and Inspections**
Directorate (SGRPID) Tel 0845 601 7597

### Wales:

**Welsh Assembly Government**
Tel 0300 0603300 or 0845 010 3300
www.wales.gov.uk

**Department for Rural Affairs**
www.countryside.wales.gov.uk

### Northern Ireland:

**Northern Ireland Executive** Tel 028 9052 8400
www.northernireland.gov.uk

**Department of Agriculture and Rural**
Development Tel 0300 200 7852
www.dardni.gov.uk

### Republic of Ireland:

**Irish Government**
Tel 0761 07 4000 www.gov.ie

**Department of Agriculture, Food and the Marine** Tel 01 607 2000
www.agriculture.gov.ie

### OTHERS

**Animal Health and Veterinary Laboratories Agency** Tel 08459 33 55 77 (Use postcode search facility on website for local contacts in England and Wales) www.defra.gov.uk/ahvla
Scotland Tel 08457 741 741 or
0131 5568400

**Animal Health Disease Outbreak Information Line** Tel 0844 8844600

**British Cattle Movement Tracing System**
Tel 0845 0501234; 0845 0503456 (Wales)
www.bcms.gov.uk

**British Deer Society** Tel 01425 655434
www.bds.org.uk

**British Pig Association** Tel 01223 845100
www.britishpigs.org

**British Sheep Dairying Association**
www.sheepdairying.com

**British Trust for Conservation Volunteers**
Tel 01302 388 883 www.btcv.org.uk

**British Veterinary Association**
Tel 020 7636 6541 www.bva.co.uk

**British Wool Marketing Board**
Tel 01274 688666   www.britishwool.org.uk

**Compulsory Scrapie Flocks Scheme Helpline**
Tel 0845 6014858

**CADW (Welsh historic environment service)**
Tel 01443 336000 www.cadw.wales.gov.uk

**Countryside Council for Wales**
Tel 0845 1306229 www.ccw.gov.uk

**Country Landowners and Business Association** (CLA) Tel 020 7235 0511
www.cla.org.uk

**Crofters' Commission** Tel 01463 663439
www.crofterscommission.org.uk

**Environment Agency**
Tel 03708 506 506 (England and Wales)
www.environment-agency.gov.uk

**Farming and Wildlife Advisory Group (FWAG)**
Tel 01203 696699 www.fwag.org.uk

**Food Standards Agency** Tel 020 7276 8829
www.food.gov.uk
Scotland Tel 01224 285100;
Wales Tel 02920 678999

**Forestry Commission** Tel 0117 906 6000
(England), 0131 334 0303 (Scotland), 0300
068 0300 (Wales) www.forestry.gov.uk

**Great Britain Poultry Register**
Helpline Tel 0800 6341112
poultry.defra.gov.uk (note, no 'www' prefix)

**Health and Safety Executive**
Tel 0151 951 4000 www.hse.gov.uk

**Heritage Council** (Republic of Ireland)
Tel (056) 777 0777 www.heritagecouncil.ie

**Historic Monuments Council** (Northern Ireland)
Tel 02890 543050 www.hmcni.gov.uk

**Historic Scotland**  Tel 0131 668 8600
www.historic-scotland.gov.uk

**Humane Slaughter Association** Tel. 01582
831919 www.hsa.org.uk  info@hsa.org.uk

**International Sheep Dog Society**
Tel 01234 352672 www.isds.org.uk

**Livestock Identification**
Helpline Tel 0845 0509876

**National Fallen Stock Scheme**
Tel 0845 0548888

**National Farmers' Retail & Markets Association (FARMA)** Tel 0845 4588420
www.farma.org.uk

**National Farmers' Union** Tel 024 76858500
www.nfuonline.com

**National Sheep Association**
www.nationalsheep.org.uk

**National Trust** Tel 0844 800 1895
www.nationaltrust.org.uk

**Natural England** Tel 0845 600 3078
www.naturalengland.org.uk

**Rare Breeds Survival Trust**
Tel 024 7669 6551 www.rbst.org.uk

**Royal Society for the Prevention of Cruelty to Animals (RSPCA)** Tel 0300 1234 555
www.rspca.org.uk

**Royal Society for the Protection of Birds (RSPB)**
Tel 01767 680551 www.rspb.org.uk

**Scottish Environment Protection Agency (SEPA)** Tel 01786 457700
www.sepa.org.uk

**Scottish Society for the Prevention of Cruelty to Animals** Tel 03000 999 999
www.scottishspca.org

**Soil Association** Tel 0117 314 5000
www.soilassociation.org

**Welfare in Transit Helpline** Tel 0845 6038395

**Wildlife Trusts** Tel 01636 677711
www.wildlifetrusts.org

**Woodland Trust** Tel 01476 581135
www.woodlandtrust.org.uk

## Recommended reading

### PUBLICATIONS

**Alpaca World**
www.alpacaworldmagazine.com

**Country Smallholding**
www.countrysmallholding.com

**Farmers Guardian**
www.farmersguardian.com

**Farmers Weekly**
www.fwi.co.uk

**Home Farmer**
www.homefarmer.co.uk

**Practical Poultry**
www.practicalpoultry.com

**Smallholder**
www.smallholder.co.uk

**Your Chickens**
www.yourchickens.co.uk

## WEBSITES

**Accidental Smallholder**
www.accidentalsmallholder.net

**River Cottage** www.rivercottage.net

**The Poultry Keeper**
www.thepoultrykeeper.co.uk

**The Pig Site** www.thepigsite.com

**The Cattle Site** www.thecattlesite.com

**UK Agriculture** www.ukagriculture.com

## BOOKS

### General smallholding

**Build It! DIY Projects for Farmers, Smallholders, and Gardeners** (Good Life Press, 2008) Jacobs, Joe

**Field to Farm: The Real Smallholding Book** (Bulldozer Publishing, 2010) Acreman, David

**How to Live Off Grid** (Bantam, 2008) Rosen, Nick

**Practical Self-Sufficiency** (Dorling Kindersley, 2010) Strawbridge, Dick and James

**Surviving and Thriving on the Land** (Green Books, 2008) Laughton, Rebecca

**The New Complete Book of Self-Sufficiency** (Dorling Kindersley, 2009) Seymour, John

**The Polytunnel Book: Fruit and Vegetables All Year Round** (Frances Lincoln, 2011) Russell, Joyce and Ben

**The Practical Guide to Buying and Running a Smallholding in Wales** (University of Wales Press, 2008) Shankland, Liz

**Tools and Machinery for the Smallholder: An Essential Guide to Their Use and Maintenance** (Crowood Press, 2011) Bezzant, John

### Livestock

#### BEES

**Beekeeping for Dummies** (John Wiley & Sons, 2011) Wiscombe, David and Blackiston, Howland

**Haynes Bee Manual** (Haynes, 2011) Waring, Claire and Andrew

**Self-sufficiency Bee Keeping** (New Holland, 2009) Ryde, Joanna

#### CAMELIDS

**Caring for Llamas and Alpacas: A Health and Management Guide** (Rocky Mountain Llama Association, 2000) Hoffman, Claire and Asmus, Ingrid

**Llamas and Alpacas: A Guide To Management** (Crowood Press, 2006) Bromage, Gina

**Llamas and Alpacas: Small-Scale Camelid Herding for Pleasure and Profit** (Hobby Farms, 2009) Weaver, Sue

**Making the Most of Your Llama** (Kopacetic Ink, 1998) Beattie, Linda C.

#### CATTLE

**Beef Cattle: Keeping a Smale-Scale Herd for Pleasure and Profit** (Bow Tie Press, 2006) Larkin Hanson, Ann

**Calf rearing** (Crowood Press, 2003) Thicket, Bill, Mitchell, Dan, and Hallows, Bryan

**Calving the Cow and Care of the Calf** (Whittet Books, 2000) Straiton, Eddie

**Caring for Cows** (Whittet Books, 1991) Porter, Valerie, and Seymour, Sally

**Cattle Ailments - Recognition and Treatment** (Whittet Books, 2002) Straiton, Eddie

**Getting Started with Beef and Dairy Cattle** (Storey Books, 2005) Smith Thomas, Heather

**Home Dairy: Keeping a House Cow, Goat or Sheep & How to Make Cheese, Yoghurt and Other Dairy Products** (Aird Books, 2011) Cliff, Ann

**The Dexter Cow and Cattle Keeping on a Small Scale** (Faber, 1954) Thrower, Rayner

**Traditional Cattle Breeds and How to Keep Them** (Farming Books and Videos, 2004) King, Peter

#### GOATS

**Goat Health and Welfare** (Crowood Press, 2006) Harwood, David

**Goat Husbandry** (Faber and Faber, 1993) Mackenzie, David

**Goat Keeping** (Interpet Publishing, 2009) Parkinson, Terry and Clarke, John

**Practical Goatkeeping** (Crowood Press, 2001) Mowlem, Alan

**Starting with Goats** (Broad Leys Publishing, 2006) Thear, Katie

**The New Goat Handbook** (Barrons, 1989) Jaudas, Ulrich

#### PIGS

**Haynes Pig Manual** (Haynes) 2011, Shankland, Liz

**Managing Pig Health and the Treatment of Disease** (5M Enterprises, 1997) Muirhead, M. and Alexander, Thomas J.L.

**Pig Ailments - Recognition and Treatment** (Crowood Press, 2005) White, Mark

**Small-Scale Outdoor Pig Breeding** (Crowood, 2011) Scudamore, Wendy

**The Whole Hog: Exploring the Extraordinary Potential of Pigs** (Profile Books, 2005) Watson, Lyall

#### POULTRY

**Backyard Chickens and Other Poultry**

(Right Way, 2011) Harrison, John

**Chickens: The Essential Guide to Choosing and Keeping Happy, Healthy Hens** (Kyle, 2012) Baldwin, Suzie

**Choosing and Keeping Chickens** (Bounty Books, 2007) Graham, Chris

**Diseases of Free-range Poultry** (Whittet Books, 2009) Roberts, Victoria

**Ducks and Geese: A Guide to Management** (Crowood Press, 1991)

**Haynes Chicken Manual** (Haynes, 2010) Beeken, Laurence

**Incubation: A Guide to Hatching and Rearing** (Broad Leys Publishing, 1997) Thear, Katie

**Starting with Chickens** (Broad Leys Publishing, 1999) Thear, Katie

**Starting with Turkeys** (Broad Leys Publishing, 2006) Thear, Katie

**The Chicken Health Handbook** (Storey, 2008) Damerow, Gail

**Keeping Quail: A Guide to Domestic and Commercial Management** (Broad Leys Publishing, 2005) Thear, Katie

#### SHEEP

**An Introduction to Keeping Sheep** (Good Life Press, 2007) Upton, Jane and Soden, Denis

**A Manual of Lambing Techniques** (Crowood Press, 2003) Winter, Agnes and Hill, Cicely

**Lameness in Sheep** (Crowood Press, 2004) Winter, Agnes

**Sheep Health, Husbandry and Disease: A Photographic Guide** (Crowood Press, 2011) Winter, Agnes, and Phythian, Clare

**Starting with Sheep** (Broad Leys Publishing, 2003) Castell, Mary

**The Modern Shepherd** (Farming Press, 2002) Brown, Dave, and Meadowcroft, Sam

**The Sheep Book for Smallholders** (Good Life Press, 2009) Tyne, Tim

#### OTHER SPECIES

**Ostrich Farming** (Beech Publishing House, 1998) Batty, Joseph

**The Ostrich: Biology, Production and Health** (CABI Publishing, 1999) Deeming, D. Charles

**The Emu Farmer's Handbook: Commercial Farming Methods for Emus, Ostriches and Rheas** (Hancock House Publishing, 1998) Minnaar, Phillip and Maria

**Domestic Water Buffalo** (South Asia Books, 1991) Fahimuddin, M.

**Wild Boar in Britain** (Whittet Books, 2003) Goulding, Martin

**Wild Boar in Europe** (Konemann UK, 2006) Cabanau, Laurent

# INDEX